GARDENING AMERICA

Regional and Historical Influences in the Contemporary Garden

Ogden Tanner

VIKING STUDIO BOOKS

VIKING STUDIO BOOKS
Published by the Penguin Group
Viking Penguin, a division of Penguin Books USA Inc.
40 West 23rd Street,
New York, New York 10010, U.S.A.
Penguin Books Ltd, 27 Wrights Lane,
London W8 5TZ, England
Penguin Books Australia Ltd, Ringwood,
Victoria, Australia
Penguin Books Canada Ltd, 2801 John Street,
Markham, Ontario, Canada L3R 1B4
Penguin Books (N.Z.) Ltd, 182-190 Wairau Road,
Auckland 10, New Zealand

Penguin Books Ltd, Registered Offices:
Harmondsworth, Middlesex, England

First published in 1990 by Viking Penguin,
a division of Penguin Books USA Inc.
Published simultaneously in Canada

10 9 8 7 6 5 4 3 2 1

Illustration credits appear on page 255.

Library of Congress Cataloging in Publication Data
Tanner, Ogden.
Gardening America: regional and historical
influences in the contemporary garden/Ogden Tanner.
p. cm.
Bibliography:p. 244–45   Includes index.
1. Gardens—United States—Design.
2. Gardens—United States—Pictorial works.
3. Gardening—United States.   I. Title.
SB466.U6T36   1989   88-20519
712.5 0973—dc19
ISBN 0-670-82240-X

Printed in Singapore
Set in the United States of America
Editor: Sarah Kirshner
Designed by Kathleen Westray and Ed Sturmer
Production Manager: Michelle Hauser
Photo Research: Roseann Martinez

*To own a bit of
ground, to scratch
it with a hoe, to
plant seeds, and watch
the renewal of life—
this is the commonest
delight of the race,
the most satisfactory
thing a man can do.*

CHARLES DUDLEY WARNER

Contents

Introduction

A PASSION for gardening is sweeping America. Not since the Victory Garden days of the 1940s have so many Americans gotten their hands into the good earth. According to a Gallup poll conducted each year for the National Gardening Association, members of seventy million households—78 percent of all households—in the United States engage in some form of gardening. That means more of us garden than swim, jog, or play tennis. Collectively we spend more than seventeen billion dollars a year on our favorite pastime, and that figure appears to be increasing substantially every year.

Gardeners are a diverse crowd. It used to be that people took up gardening after they hit the age of fifty, when the kids were grown and suddenly there was more free time. But today's gardeners come in all ages, shapes, and sizes. The most fervent converts these days are between the ages of thirty and fifty, people who are settling down, buying homes, raising children. This new crop of gardeners includes as many men as women, and they live all over the country.

As diverse as the people who garden are the reasons why they garden. Some people grow flowers to add color to their

Brilliant perennials in Fred and Mary Ann McGourty's Connecticut garden.

yards and to have bouquets for indoors; others grow vegetables or fruit to savor the unsurpassable flavor of homegrown, freshly picked tomatoes or corn or peas. Herbs have captured the fancy of still others who use them for cooking, for dried arrangements or wreaths, or for creating fragrant potpourris. An increasing number of gardeners grow plants native to their part of the country—a practice that is not only rewarding in itself but that minimizes maintenance since the plants are well adapted to the climate. Some homeowners garden for economic reasons; attractive landscaping has been found to increase property values and resale prices of homes.

Whatever reason one has for gardening, it is an enjoyable activity that provides both physical and psychological benefits. In addition to exercise and fresh air, gardening brings most people a feeling of serenity, a certain peace of mind

in an uncertain world. Not least of all, it gives us a sense of place, a feeling of connection to the land, of rootedness. And roots are what this book is about.

Over the course of nearly four centuries, Americans have tried to put down roots in many different places, in many different ways. The gardens that have blossomed from them are marvelously—sometimes bewilderingly—varied, ranging from nostalgic copies of English or Italian landscapes to stunning originals that seem to spring from the forests, mountains, and prairies themselves.

It has been said that gardens are people's windows on the natural world. What a person sees through a window, of course, depends on what is there and, often, on what he or she wants to see. The first settlers in the New World saw a wilderness that had to be tamed and they tamed it, laying

out an orderly, familiar kind of garden that provided a sort of buffer zone between them and nature in the raw, a comforting picture of man's control over the unknown.

After a long succession of changing attitudes and fads, brightened a half century ago by the beginnings of gardens more sensibly suited to modern needs, there seems to be emerging today the exact opposite of the prototypical American garden. It is a new kind of garden, a new kind of picture, one that tries—through wildflowers, grasses, and other native plants—to recapture the original beauty of the natural scene which, in the course of developing their country, Americans now realize they have almost managed to wipe out.

On the following pages we will look at gardens and plants that are particularly revealing of their regions and eras from coast to coast, landscapes that trace the changing patterns of American gardening and American life. By and large they are gardens that make the most of their local climates and topographies, their cultural heritage, their native as well as naturalized plants—gardens that in varying degrees capture what Alexander Pope called the "genius of the place." In short, these are gardens that themselves have roots, that seem to belong where they are.

We hope this book adds to Americans' understanding of where their gardens may be going, as well as where they have been.

All across America, gardens are rooted in a traditional love of beauty. From far left: wisteria in Charleston, South Carolina; an old lilac tree and hollyhocks on Mackinac Island, Michigan; a garden gate in California.

The Roots of American Gardening

"There came a smell off the shore like the smell of a garden. . . ."
—John Winthrop, 1630

TODAY THE native American landscape has become an inspiration for many gardeners, but in the beginning it received decidedly mixed reviews from European newcomers.

After a seemingly endless voyage on a small, creaking wooden ship, the green coast of New England appeared to John Winthrop, governor of the Massachusetts Bay Colony; as a God-given vision—a "garden" that he could even savor with his nose.

To other arrivals in New England, raised among the open fields and hedgerows of old England, the heavily forested new land was anything but a garden; rather it was forbidding country to settle and difficult to farm, full of swamps and rocks, Indians and wolves. A "hideous, howling wilderness," one Boston minister described it on a journey inland in 1694.

It was this wild landscape—and its equally wild and dramatically beautiful counterparts in the prairies, deserts, and mountains farther west—that was eventually to shape American gardens over the centuries to come.

It cannot be said that appreciating the natural beauty of the American landscape was uppermost in the earliest settlers' minds. The main job at hand was to carve a living out of the land—in an early loggers' phrase, to "let daylight into the swamp." And so the tall trees of nature's garden fell before the axe, to be used for firewood and building timber, to make room for houses and farms.

The gardens of the earliest settlers are re-created at Massachusetts' Plimoth Plantation.

In such a setting, it is not surprising that the first cultivated gardens were practical ones. The settlers brought with them seeds, roots, and memories from home, using Elizabethan cottage gardens as models in laying out their modest plots. Vegetables and herbs traditional to the old country were planted, along with native corn, beans, tobacco, and other crops whose culture the settlers learned from friendly native Indians.

Though almost every house had a few flowers—old favorites like roses, or wild violets and mayflowers transplanted from the woods—the first American gardens were primarily designed for "meate and medicine" needed for kitchen and sick room, in an era when a lot of time was spent in both. Vegetables, grown in a plot near the house fenced to keep out both domestic and wild animals, included old standbys like peas, lettuce, melons, artichokes, onions, and leeks. Especially favored were turnips, beets, carrots, cabbages, and squashes, which had the bulk to fill hungry stomachs, and, in the absence of refrigeration, also stored well to provide more winter meals. Interestingly, tomatoes—by far the most popular vegetable today, with 85 percent of home vegetable gardeners growing them—were unknown to the early settlers. Though

Perennials, lilacs, boxwood, and wisteria grace the gardens at Hawthorne's "House of the Seven Gables" in Salem, Massachusetts.

first cultivated as a food by the Aztecs of Mexico, and brought back to Spain by Cortes around 1520, tomatoes were long thought by Europeans and Americans to be sensuous, evil, or downright poisonous. They were not widely eaten in North America until the mid-1800s.

Early American gardens were not always neat; vegetables were often mixed at random with flowers and herbs, though fruits like strawberries, currants, and gooseberries were usually grown separately. Apples and other larger fruits were given small orchards of their own, and corn, beans, and pumpkins were usually relegated to open fields.

There were no modern drugs in those days, and most medical therapy was based on plants. To minister to family ills, the Colonial housewife prepared hot, soothing teas of chamomile, sage, and wintergreen. Herbal plasters, salves, and lotions eased the pains of childbirth or treated toothaches, coughs, or cuts. There were even special herbs used for laying out the dead. Some of the recipes were formidable: "For wind Collick, take Summer Savory, Angelica, Sweet Tansy; and Elecampane; for back pains, make a syrup of Borage or Comphrey and add Brandy and Gunpowder to taste."

BEFORE LONG, the crude plots of Plimoth Plantation and other settlements evolved into more presentable dooryard gardens like those in Ipswich, Sturbridge, and other trim New England towns. In most villages, fencing was required by law to keep out stray animals, giving birth to those American trademarks, the picket fence and post-and-rail fence. Successive waves of immigrants planted lilacs by their doors as reminders of their European homes. Here and there one can still glimpse an overgrown lilac bush in front of an old house—a sweet, haunting reminder of the past.

In early America, a garden was a woman's pride—and largely a woman's work. At left: a lady in period costume tends to diagonal rows of vegetables and flowers at Old Salem, in North Carolina. Below: a Norwegian-American garden at Old World Wisconsin.

FOR A long time gardening was essentially cottage agriculture. By the mid-eighteenth century, however, prosperous farmers and merchants could afford decorative gardens for pleasure as well, including plots that featured tulips, hollyhocks, and other colorful flowers imported from abroad. They lavished as much care on their plants as modern gardeners do—perhaps more, for in those days of limited travel, people spent most of their time at home, and much of that enjoying their own backyards.

Again, the colonists turned to the old country for inspiration. In the restorations of Virginia's Williamsburg and North Carolina's Tryon Palace one can clearly see the influence of English gardens, laid out on formal axes and embellished with geometrical parterres, planted in flowers outlined by boxwood like their counterparts across the Atlantic.

The most impressive gardens of the late eighteenth and early nineteenth centuries belonged to the great plantations of the middle Atlantic and southern states, especially Virginia—Thomas Jefferson's Monticello, George Washington's Mount Vernon, Westover, Gunston Hall, Stratford

Seasonal flowers, edged in clipped dwarf holly, adorn an eighteenth-century English garden at Tryon Palace, in New Bern, North Carolina.

Hall, and others. The plantations—larger ones covered as much as 10,000 acres and were served by upwards of 200 slaves—were self-sufficient fiefdoms, worlds of their own. Not unlike their prototypes in feudal England, they were directed by landed gentlemen who thought of themselves as English squires, and many of whom were not only skilled estate managers and farmers but avid horticulturists.

The Deep South boasted other great country seats, like Middleton Place outside Charleston, South Carolina. Started in 1741, and taking a hundred slaves nearly a decade to complete, Middleton Place is regarded as the first major example of landscape design in America, and still one of the finest. Henry Middleton and his heirs were ardent gardeners and plant collectors, ordering large shipments of seeds and plants from suppliers in England. By the end of the century they were planting many ornamental species obtained from abroad, including some of the first Oriental camellias and azaleas seen in America, for plant hunters had begun to comb the wilds of South America and the Far East and commercial nurserymen were promoting their finds.

Colonial Willamsburg, the famed restoration of the Virginia Colony's capital, is also known for its grandly landscaped Governor's Palace, but even more for its many lovely, smaller gardens designed in seventeenth-century Dutch-English style, with bright flowers, patterned brick walks, and formal evergreen parterres.

As it did for the Middletons, gardening became a tradition for many Colonial families, including those of more modest means. In some cases the garden was a major expression of continuity and religious faith. In an article on the Wyck garden in Philadelphia, which was lovingly tended by nine successive generations of the same Quaker family, garden historian Sandra MacKenzie Lloyd writes: "In Reuben's eyes, it was essential that parents teach their children to nurture the earth and make it fertile with vegetables and flowers. His philosophy corresponded with Quaker beliefs that the earth was a gift from God to man. Man, then, had the responsibility and pleasure of cultivating the earth for his own benefit and as a celebration of God's goodness."

Responsibility aside, gardening could also be a deep source of simple joy. Wrote Sarah Goodwin, a resident of the settlement in Portsmouth, New Hampshire, named Strawbery Banke after the abundant wild berries found along the river: "Oh the comfort, the delight I have had in my garden. I have loved my house and all my pleasant things in it, but the greatest, most solid comfort I have ever had, has been in my garden."

AS THE nineteenth century progressed, however, new fashions evolved. Chief among these was a growing Victorian penchant for the romantic and the picturesque.

Ancient live oaks draped with Spanish moss line a riverside walk at Middleton Place.

A major spokesman for the new movement was Andrew Jackson Downing. A nurseryman's son who grew up along the Hudson River in Newburgh, New York, Downing by his early twenties had earned a reputation as a landscape designer among owners of great Hudson Valley estates, as well as becoming the editor of *The Horticulturist,* a popular magazine of agrarian life. Inspired by developments in England, Downing advocated a rustic Gothic style to replace the Greek Revival houses that then dominated American taste. To landscape them appropriately, he made detailed suggestions for achieving either a "beautiful" effect with soft, curving lines, or a "picturesque" feeling with a wilder, irregular look. His book, *A Trea-*

tise on the Theory and Practice of Landscape Gardening, published in 1841, went through ten editions, the last of which appeared in 1875.

Downing's writings were devoured by a growing middle class that yearned for a touch of elegance in their houses and gardens but weren't sure how to achieve it. Andrew held the banner high: "When smiling lawns and tasteful cottages begin to embellish a country," he wrote, " we know that order and culture have been established."

Downing met a tragic and untimely death at thirty-two trying to save fellow passengers in a Hudson River boat fire, but his disciples carried on. Amid the raging eclecticism of the Victorian era, however, matters soon got out of hand. Downing's "smiling lawns"

were enthusiastically dotted with specimen trees from China or India, patterned flower beds in garish colors, curlicued furniture, gazebos, Chinese pagodas, Roman urns, wood nymphs, or iron deer. Assortments of evergreens planted to conceal the unsightly foundations of raised houses with porches evolved into "foundation plantings," a notion that was to persist long after houses rested at ground level atop sunken basements.

A love of ornate gardens, garden furniture, and sculptural accents, which swept both Europe and America during the decades of Queen Victoria's reign, has enjoyed renewed interest in the Victorian revival of recent years. Above, left: multicolored flowers laid out in carpet-bedding style. At right: a reproduction of a nineteenth-century cast-iron garden chair.

A tradition that became even more deeply ingrained was the lawn itself, which traced its ancestry to the pastoral, sheep-nibbled parklands of British country estates. For quite a while in America, too, lawns were largely playthings of the wealthy, who could employ hired hands to cut them with horse-drawn mowing machines. By the 1870s, however, the invention of a small, inexpensive reel mower allowed even owners of modest homes to spend their Sunday afternoons leveling the grass. Advertisements of the day pictured little girls in dainty frocks gaily skipping along behind the newest mowers to show just how easy it was to operate them.

Amidst the fun and games, no one suspected the lawnmower—motorized, and abetted by fertilizers, weedkillers, soil conditioners, trimmers, edgers, aerators, and dethatchers—would come to dominate American gardens and gardeners over the next hundred years. A 1987 Gallup survey conducted for the National Gardening Association showed that nearly 60 percent of all households in the United States listed "lawn care" as their major gardening activity, and they spent close to five and a half billion dollars a year on it—almost as much as they spent on landscaping, flower growing and vegetable gardening combined. No wonder that a whole new industry of lawn-care services has arisen to take the chores off homeowners' hands.

Part of the vast central greensward at Middleton Place. Before the age of lawnmowers, browsing livestock kept the grass trimmed on large estates.

A LONG WITH the Victorian penchant for broad lawns and romantic designs, different threads had been weaving their way into the fabric of American garden design. Beginning in the 1800s, a new craze for rock gardening with colorful, diminutive alpine plants was imported from England and spread among the fashion-conscious in America, with sometimes ludicrous results. (Sniffed a noted gardener, Liberty Hyde Bailey, "A rock garden is a place in which to grow plants. . . . If one is making a collection of rocks, one's pursuit is geology rather than gardening.") Serious gardeners, however, refined rock gardening to an art form, particularly in the Northeast, where it fit comfortably into the naturally rocky woodland terrain.

Still other influences on garden design came into play as the nation expanded westward. In response to the baking heat of the South and Southwest, early Spanish and French settlers had built cool, cloistered courtyard gardens, inspired by their gardens back home. Some of these courtyards can still be seen in the chain of Franciscan missions in California, and in Arizona, New Mexico, and the old French Quarter of New Orleans.

Rock gardens were among the myriad landscaping ideas nineteenth-century Americans enthusiastically imported from the Old World, where they had been inspired by a fascination for the small, brilliantly-flowered plants that hikers and botanists discovered in the Alps.

The late nineteenth and early twentieth centuries, sometimes referred to as the "Country Place Era," were notable for opulent private estates, many of whose lavish landscapes are now great public gardens. Built by successful industrialists bent on showing off their good taste, most of these landscapes were copies of palatial gardens their owners had admired during frequent travels abroad. Among the most famous are Philadelphia's Longwood Gardens, originally built as a home by Pierre du Pont, with magnificent fountains rivaling those of Versailles; John Deering's Villa Vizcaya in Miami, an intricate reproduction of noble estates in the Italian hills; and William Randolph Hearst's famous San Simeon, a Hollywood version of a Renaissance palazzo reaching for the California sky.

Some of the gardens of this gilded age were magnificently done, like those of Dumbarton Oaks in Washington, D.C., and Abby Aldrich Rockefeller's garden near Bar Harbor in Maine. Both these gardens were designed by Beatrix Farrand, America's first major female landscape architect. Other grand gardens, quite different in style, included Winterthur in Delaware and many estates along the Hudson River that drew inspiration from a back-to-nature fad that had started to sweep the country.

For three centuries American gardens had been largely adaptations of European ideas. Then, beginning in

"Landscaping is not a complex and difficult art to be practiced only by high priests," wrote Thomas Church. "It is logical, down-to-earth, and aimed at making your plot of ground produce exactly what you want and need from it. . . . It must be a green oasis where memories of [the] bumper-to-bumper ride from work will be erased. . . ." "Gardens are for people," he concluded, and the nation enthusiastically agreed.

In California in particular, the seeds fell on fertile ground. A sunny, dry climate, similar to that of the Mediterranean along the coast, had long encouraged people to enjoy the outdoors. Moreover, in such a climate almost anything would grow, year-round, including not only a wealth of native plants but hundreds of exotic species that Californians began importing from the warmer regions of Asia, Australia, and the Mediterranean itself. Unrestrained by eastern notions of conservatism, westerners embraced brilliant colors and bold forms when designing their gardens.

Along the same guidelines that directed modern architecture, form began to follow function rather than be imposed on it, freeing gardens to be shaped by their owners' needs, the nature of their local climates and sites, and the variety of local plant life.

The beginnings of the California style can be seen in this early San Francisco garden designed by Thomas Church.

A particular target of the California school was the old notion of foundation planting, which was not always suited to the new style of living and often grew up to block light and views. Church and others moved most of the planting farther out, where it could serve to enlarge and define an outdoor "room" in front of the house as well as in back—an entrance garden that would provide a sense of enclosure and a welcome at the front door.

A major influence that coincided nicely with such ideas, particularly on the West Coast, was the rediscovery of ancient Japanese gardens. These were reproduced on private estates and in public gardens, and their distinctive principles of design were imaginatively incorporated into modern gardens of more modest size as well.

Today gardeners in North America are no longer limited to a choice of "formal" or "picturesque," but can select from an almost unlimited array of garden types— outdoor-living gardens, woodland gardens, perennial gardens, water gardens, drought-resistant gardens, gardens of ornamental grasses or evergreens. The choices are legion, and continue to proliferate.

Rapidly growing in popularity today are "low maintenance" gardens, achieved by using ground covers and paving instead of grass that has to be mowed; slow-growing, well-behaved species of trees and shrubs; and mulched beds, container plants, and other labor-saving techniques. Often combined with a desire for low maintenance is a growing interest in ecology and conservation, and a per-

In a Japanese garden on the West Coast, water from a bamboo pipe drips musically into an ornamental stone bowl among azaleas and rocks. Such artful compositions, in the Japanese style, of three elements in the landscape—stone, water, and plants—have strongly influenced modern American garden design.

sonal delight in observing nature at work over the changing seasons in one's own backyard. These environmental and aesthetic concerns have led to the widespread adoption of naturalistic meadow and woodland gardens, which have achieved increasing favor as an alternative to the tyranny of formal plantings and lawns.

Indeed, the newest revolution in garden design is emerging from a belated appreciation of the native landscape—and from even more powerful factors as well. Among them are increasing worries about water supplies in many regions of the country, and the realization that lawns and fancy ornamental plantings require far more water than native grasses, wildflowers, and trees, which have long adapted to local conditions of rainfall and drought. In addition, more gardeners are recognizing not only that constant applications of fertilizers, weedkillers, and pesticides are expensive and time-consuming, but that they can kill songbirds and beneficial insects, contaminate ground water, and upset the ecological balance of estuaries and lakes. Yet another factor is the economic pressure that puts both husbands and wives to work, leaving them with little inclination to spend their few free hours each week laboriously tending to their yards.

A blend of Oriental and natural styles is reflected in this garden, where irises bloom around a shallow pool set off by stones chosen for their decorative striations and beautifully rounded shapes. The plants provide graceful counterpoints with their tall clumps of fountaining leaves.

Many of those who have experimented with the new approach to gardening, moreover, have found it basically more satisfying, not just because gardens of native plants require less work after the plantings have become established, but because they present a more interesting natural panorama through the seasons, attracting birds, butterflies, and other wildlife to animate the scene.

STILL OTHER influences, including continuing urbanization and crowding, promise to have a growing impact on American garden design, demanding more ingenious use of dwindling land. One reason for the popularity of "wild" gardens, in fact, is that their use of high meadow grasses and screening shrubs provides a greater feeling of privacy and space on a small suburban lot than is afford-

ed by a naked lawn open to neighbors and traffic on the street.

The growth of condominiums and clustered housing, brought on by high land and construction costs, is also leading to a distinctly twentieth-cen-

Native plants are increasingly recognized for their beauty and toughness. Above, left: wildflowers grown from a commercial seed mix. Above, right: lacy patterns of field grasses and sumacs in a meadow garden near Detroit.

tury American pattern: small backyard or balcony gardens overlooking larger communal open spaces which, when well designed, can bring back the pleasures of the old village green or central park. Maintained by homeowners' associations, these shared landscapes provide convenient, traffic-free places to stroll and smell the flowers, as well as to play tennis or swim in a community pool.

The traditional garden, in fact, while becoming more private is becoming more public, too, and this may be the most significant trend of all. It can be seen in cities across the country where community gardens have sprung up, allowing neighbors to raise their own fresh vegetables and flowers on vacant lots, in the process sharing new interests, new friendships, and a new sense of human worth. It can be seen in the gardenlike parks and plazas of corporate headquarters and shopping malls, where workers bask or socialize in the sun during their lunch breaks. It can be seen in immensely popular "people parks" like Portland, Oregon's play-in fountains and Manhattan's vest-pocket Paley and Greenacre parks, where oases of greenery and cascading water open up the dense, often oppressive, fabric of urban life.

Whether or not such shared gardens are the wave of the future, they—and the vitality of a new, native regionalism sprouting around the country—are welcome developments in the history of American garden design.

City dwellers appreciate urban gardens of different kinds. Below, left: children at play in a "people's fountain" in downtown Portland, Oregon. Below, right: a young gardener in a community garden, sponsored by the city of Chicago on a vacant lot.

The Northeast

2

IN THE country's oldest settled region, one can still see clearly gardening traditions inherited from Europe, and further shaped by the rugged nature of the climate and the land.

Faced with the cold, snowy winters of New England and New York and surrounded by a wilderness of seemingly endless forests, early settlements were frugally clustered, well-ordered, and compact, as were the houses and gardens of which they were comprised. For a long time the settlers were basically harvesters of trees, preoccupied with clearing them for farms, and using the wood for building and heating their homes and erecting fences against wandering livestock. They were also unwilling harvesters of rocks, prying endless crops of glacial boulders from the shallow soil and piling them into stone walls—the now well-loved trademarks that stitch the region together.

By the nineteenth century much of New England had been wrested from forest and laboriously converted into farmland. But as more and more farmers gave up and moved to the richer, deeper soils of the Midwest, the forest gradually returned, and continues to do so wherever fields are not cut back. In contrast with their ancestors, to whom the forest was both obstacle and economy, many gardeners in the region today have gratefully accepted this persistent green canopy, along with the rocks and rills beneath it, as a natural, scenic gift—an opportunity to create gardens that evoke the beauty of the land itself.

In a woodland garden in New Canaan, Connecticut, sunlight illuminates the greenery.

While the Northeast, with its ample rainfall, is naturally lush and green, plants grown there must be hardy to survive: the growing season is short and winters can be severe. Spring is slow in coming, but when it does the woods bloom with dogwoods and, later, mountain laurel. Woodland wildflowers—Dutchman's breeches, trout lilies, bloodroot, foamflowers, ladyslipper orchids—add color closer to the ground. Autumn sets the foliage of sugar maples and other trees ablaze; entire hillsides glow with oranges, reds, russets, and golds, the colors often intensified by a backdrop of

brilliant blue sky. After the leaves have gone, the countryside sleeps beneath a blanket of snow.

Gardens in the Northeast, then, are largely spring and summer affairs, though, as we shall see, there are ways to extend the calendar of interest year-

Favorite flowers of northeastern gardeners include wild roses (above), which thrive everywhere along the coast, and the distinctive blooms of yellow ladyslippers, or moccasin flowers (right), native orchids that grow naturally in damp woods. Varieties of native and Oriental primroses, often used in low wet areas around streams, are set off in the picture at far right by the giant leaves of petasites, a native of Japan.

round. Country gardens are often bounded by stone walls and are typically viewed against a background of green forests or an expanse of green lawn. Northeastern gardeners plant herb gardens, charming dooryard gardens, and exuberant mixtures of annuals and perennials, all stemming from Colonial traditions. The cool climate is especially hospitable to delphiniums, astilbes, columbines, bleeding heart, primroses, lupines, ligularia, and thalictrum. Shady gardens may hold hostas, impatiens, and tuberous begonias. In brightly sunny coastal gardens, sun-loving achillea, day lilies, blanketflowers, zinnias, and coreopsis spread their brilliant blossoms wide under the sky.

Far left, top: an island of perennials in the green of a Connecticut lawn; bottom: rocks, water, evergreens, and a large urn in a garden in Maine. Below, left: tuberous begonias and ferns; right: the delicate blossoms of sweet peas.

A Heritage of Herbs

FOLLOWING Elizabethan precedents, the simple dooryard gardens of early settlements were soon elaborated into patterns that exploited the decorative aspects of herbs, many of which were prized for the distinctive colors and textures of their leaves. These included "gray" or "silver" gardens of artemisias, lamb's ears, dittany, lavender, woolly mint, and silver thyme, as well as intricate "knot" gardens composed of bands of different colored foliage interwoven in geometrical designs.

While herbal home remedies have largely been replaced by modern medicine, herb gardens continue to be popular, particularly in the Northeast. Herb gardens are satisfying not only for their historical associations and for the natural scents and flavorings they provide, but for the sheer, old-fashioned beauty they afford.

Herb gardens take many forms. One favorite style is the knot garden, a formal style that has been popular since Shakespeare's time in Elizabethan England. In a knot garden, herbs with varying foliage colors are planted in intricate interwoven patterns. Herbs are also planted in geometric beds, often with a sundial or other ornament in the center. While such gardens are attractive, they require constant clipping and weeding to keep them that way. Gardeners without the time or inclination for such painstaking upkeep grow herbs in less formal ways, often interspersing them with flowers or vegetables in ordinary garden beds.

At Sundial Herb Garden in Higganum, Connecticut, a raised knot garden (below) interweaves strands of dark green germander and blue-green rue. The main garden (bottom, right and far right) features a central sundial in a bed of lamb's ears. In a smaller Connecticut garden (top, right), herbs are enclosed by an old picket fence.

Inviting Dooryards

THE MOST characteristic of early American gardens were beds handily placed outside the door for vegetables and herbs on which the colonists depended for their everyday needs. Often contained by logs or boards, raised for drainage, and neatly divided by paths, the beds were planted with seeds or cuttings of favorite household plants brought over from the old country, sometimes interspersed with native species whose uses the settlers learned from their neighbors, the Indians.

Every Puritan housewife knew, as the seventeenth-century English herbalist and physician John Parkinson wrote, "what Herbes and Fruits were fit, eyther for meate or medicine, for Use or Delight." And she could grow almost everything her family required: not only the basic ingredients of everyday dishes but flavorings, garnishes; and "sallets" to accompany them; remedies for all manner of ills; nosegays for freshening the air of rooms; repellents for mice, bugs, and snakes; dyes to color homemade woolens and the bristly flower heads of teasel for teasing up their naps.

In addition to such utilitarian considerations, every Colonial garden had a few flowers cultivated for their beauty alone, and for the hospitable note they offered visiting neighbors and friends. It was from this early American pride in home that the widespread notion of a welcoming front yard evolved.

One of America's oldest dooryard gardens (far left) is that of the Whipple House in Ipswich, Massachusetts, built in 1640, where plants were chosen for their practical uses as well as their visual appeal. A Nantucket cottage (above) is framed by an arbor of pink climbing roses, with more red roses at the door.

Raised beds are popular today for containing plants and bringing them up where they're easier to appreciate and tend. The idea, however, is hardly new. Edged by wooden planks, and arranged in formal patterns separated by paths, such beds are dominant features at the House of Seven Gables in Salem, Massachusetts, where they display Colonial favorites like tulips, marigolds, pansies, scarlet runner beans, baby's breath, and Bouncing Bet. The gardens are seen here in three views: in late May (far left), in late September (left), and in early October (above).

Colorful Perennial Gardens

LONGTIME favorites, particularly in the Northeast, have been gardens built around beds and borders of colorful mixed flowers displayed for simple visual delight. Partly inspired by old English gardens, many contemporary designs reflect a current trend to perennial plants, which can be mixed and matched to provide season-long beauty year after year.

While some homeowners are content with a burst of tulips and daffodils in spring, leaving gardens largely green the rest of the year, knowledgeable gardeners plan a more comprehensive calendar of color, using plants and varieties that bloom at different times to provide a continuous show. To such gardeners, the challenge is to extend the season of interest for as long as possible, starting with snowdrops and other small bulbs that flower as early as March, often poking unexpectedly through the snow. Although the perennial garden reaches its

Near left: tall, graceful delphiniums. Left, above: a perennial border with feathery astilbes, tall verbascums, and delphiniums. Left, below: shade-tolerant hostas, like these with cream-edged foliage, produce attractive flower spikes but are even more valued for their bold rosettes of leaves.

peak bloom in summer, gardeners can ensure color from spring to fall by planning carefully. Still another way to extend the show in the garden is to include plants that offer something nice to look at all year—even in winter—including shrub dogwoods with bright red stems, and tall tufts of ornamental grasses whose brownish yellow leaves remain handsome until March, when the cycle of garden flowering resumes.

An example of the traditional perennial garden at its best is the one developed over the years by Fred and Mary Ann McGourty of Norfolk, Connecticut. It is a summer-long symphony of color, carefully orchestrated against a background of crisp green lawns and old stone walls. In one part of this garden, tall pink *Phlox paniculata* blooms with golden coreopsis, sunny yellow lilies, rich scarlet beebalm, and crisp white campanulas and shasta daisies. Another brilliant border blends carmine-red astilbes with blue delphiniums, pink echinacea, and pink alliums.

Another approach to perennial gardens is to include beds of flowers in carefully planned beds enclosed by walls, fences, or hedges that define the spaces as outdoor "rooms." The feeling of a room can be further implied by installing an arbor or pergola with vines trained up and over the structure to create a "roof," by adding a piece of decorative statuary or other ornament, and by otherwise furnishing the "room" with benches, chairs, and perhaps a table for outdoor dining. A large garden can have several such rooms, adapted to different uses and growing conditions in different locations. One room might contain a shade garden, for example, with hostas, astilbes, and other shade-tolerant plants; another room might be devoted to sun-lovers like achillea and rudbeckia.

Below, left: a stunning bed of perennials in a Maine garden catches the morning light. Below, right: another garden set off by a stone wall and a decorative urn. Right: symmetrical plant beds in a traditional New England garden.

. . . .

*At Hillside Gardens in Norfolk, Connecticut,
Fred and Mary Ann McGourty maintain a
showcase of perennials, propagating and selling
outstanding varieties from their barn. One of their
special loves is Sedum 'Autumn Joy,' which turns
rosy red in August (above). Others are Ligularia
'The Rocket' (left), well named for fiery yellow
spires that explode six feet above the ground. At
right: a view from the garden over an old stone
wall into the well-tended woodland beyond.*

Beautiful Backyards

As TOWNS grew into cities, outdoor space became more precious, and what there was of it was often put to utilitarian use, accommodating laundry lines, garbage bins, outhouses, carriage houses, or storage sheds. Nevertheless, many new urbanites were determined to cling to their rural past, even if their gardens had to be limited to a few geraniums and marigolds in a windowbox or some shrubs or English ivy by the front door.

Backyards, too, were used to grow flowers and vegetables, at least where surrounding buildings allowed enough sunshine to penetrate during the day. Long before the advent of air conditioning, city dwellers put chairs outside their kitchen doors on stifling summer nights; there they would relax after dinner, hoping for a cool breeze and a glimpse of stars in the night sky.

Seen through archways from back service alleys (left), two small yards in Boston's Beacon Hill section have been transformed into attractive and useful gardens with plantings, furnishings, and pavings of brick. The high back wall of another garden (below) is nicely broken up by a spiral stair and wrought-iron balcony where potted hibiscuses and smaller flowers are placed to take advantage of the sun.

While there have long been gardens in cities, it is only in more recent times that the notion has spread of using urban backyards, balconies, and even rooftops as decorative outdoor rooms for relaxation, dining, or play. Examples can be seen in many urban neighborhoods today, including the handsome nineteenth-century townhouses of Boston's Beacon Hill, where owners have created an array of gardens out of a modicum of space.

These tiny courtyard gardens are often paved with brick, and incorporate brick-sided raised beds, sometimes terraced into two or more levels. Wrought-iron furniture, decorative urns and planters, and small pieces of statuary complete the setting. Beacon Hill gardeners grow small shrubs and trees—rhododendrons and dwarf conifers, for example—to give the garden basic structure. They add color with tulips and daffodils in spring, pots of annuals (impatiens, geraniums, petunias, pansies) in summer, and chrysanthemums in fall. Hidden from view of the street, these diminutive gardens are private, quiet retreats, pleasant places to escape the bustle of the city outside.

Many of the gardens in Beacon Hill are hardly more than 10 feet wide. One small area (above) is visually broadened by whitewashed walls, circular paving, and a curved, raised planting bed. Another (below) is enlivened by flowering shrubs and a fountain pool. A rooftop garden (far right) uses movable containers for its plantings, and latticed fences for privacy.

Gardens by the Sea

MANY OF New England's first gardens were built in settlements near the sea, on which the inhabitants depended for their livelihoods in fishing, whaling, or shipbuilding, as well as for most of their travel and trade. Perhaps no picture is more romantically associated with the region than that of a rose-covered Cape Cod cottage adorned by a white picket fence out front and fishing floats and lobster pots behind.

It was to the seaside that many Americans first turned for their summer pleasures as well. Some of the earliest weekend and vacation homes in the region were the tiny cottages that wealthy merchants and whaling captains of Nantucket town built for themselves in Siasconset, a cliffside retreat at the island's eastern end only a few miles away.

Seaside gardens have always had a special magic, blossoming with colors

Behind a summer cottage in Maine's Northeast Harbor (far left), a bed of brilliant perennials curves down to the waters of Somes Sound. Red and pink climbing roses (above) frame a welcoming pink doorway on Nantucket.

At a waterfront home in Guilford, Connecticut, white-flowered yuccas and pale yellow daylilies tolerate the salt air of Long Island Sound (above). A patchwork of heathers and granite adorns a garden in Freeport, Maine (right).

that seem more intense than their inland counterparts. Part of the secret is the climate—often-brilliant summer days, with blue skies and scudding clouds, tempered by cool nights and washed by ocean air, with frequent fogs and heavy morning dews providing ample moisture for the plants. Another part of the charm, certainly, is the backdrop of the coast itself, with its picturesque harbors and rocky views. The rest is the work of gardeners who love flowers, and who treasure their summers in the sun.

Seaside gardens in the Northeast are usually full of brilliant colors—pastels tend to look washed out in bright sunlight. Especially popular are deep golden achillea, pink armeria, yellow coreopsis, steel blue echinops, day lilies in a host of warm shades, black-eyed Susans, blanketflowers, rosy purple lythrum, yellow thermopsis, and sparkling white shasta daisies. Artemisias and other silver-leaved plants also hold up well in strong sun, and offer some visual relief from the intense, hot colors. Sun-loving annuals have a place in these gardens, too. Marigolds, nasturtiums, snapdragons, and ageratum all thrive in seaside flower beds.

Seaside gardens in New England are often notable for the intensity of their colors, as seen in the two perennial borders on this page. The moist fogs and morning dews of the ocean climate seem to promote brilliant color in the flowers. In a third garden (far right), daylilies, daisies, and zinnias are displayed against a background of blue ocean and dark green firs.

Gardening on the Rocks

AMERICANS didn't invent rock gardens; along with many other ideas, they first imported the notion from England. But they can boast an astonishing array of rock gardens, of all sizes and shapes. This may be attributed to Yankee ingenuity and to the fact that the East Coast, appropriately, has a lot of rocks.

While the glacial garbage left by the last ice age was a source of woe to earlier settlers, who had to pile the boulders into stone walls before they could plow the soil, it has provided modern homeowners with endless chances to create charming garden scenes, and to experiment with a variety of small plants that are ideally suited to the modest dimensions of the average lot.

Indeed, many rock-garden species don't require a rock garden at all, but can be planted in pockets of soil in an unmortared stone wall, or in soil-filled crevices between the stones of a terrace or patio. Some of these diminutive

In Lincoln Foster's rock garden in Connecticut (far left), mountain phlox, marsh marigolds and globeflowers. In Frank Cabot's garden in Cold Spring, New York (center), alpine flowers flourish in raised stone beds. In Ted Child's garden in Norfolk, Connecticut, gravel paths and evergreens form a setting for colorful flower drifts.

plants are exquisite enough to be used for "trough gardens" arranged in shallow containers of lightweight concrete. Intended for viewing up close, trough gardens make fine showcases for smaller jewels that would get lost in the main garden.

Where good imitations of nature are hard to achieve, many gardeners have found that a simpler, and frankly manmade, solution is to build a raised, free-standing bed of smaller stones or heavy timbers, and grow the plants in both the top and sides. Another ap-

proach is to plant them in and above a retaining wall of stones or timbers set against a hill.

Special features of rock gardens are the low-growing but often brilliantly colored alpine species—saxifrages, sedums, and sempervivums, for example—that were originally collected from the mountainous regions of the world by plant explorers. Adapted to windswept altitudes and poor, rocky soil, alpines demand perfect drainage and cool depth for their long, moisture-seeking roots; they cannot long

tolerate rich soil, dampness, heat, or humidity. Fortunately, many difficult alpine species have close cousins that require less pampering. There are also a number of more familiar lowland plants that seem to fit naturally into rock gardens, among them small flowering bulbs, herbs, ferns, succu-

In a woodland clearing on Frank Cabot's estate (far left), a rivulet angles down through rocks and azaleas to a man-made pond outlined in naturalistic curves. In Pomfret, Connecticut (below), an airy garden pavilion overlooks a mounded island adorned with rock-garden plants.

lents, dwarf azaleas, and other shrubs. Low-growing perennials such as moss pinks, primroses, perennial candytuft, basket-of-gold, draba, aubrieta, arabis, trilliums, gentians, and other perennial flowers are also well-suited to the rock-garden scene.

One of the rock gardens shown here is on a hilltop near Cold Spring, New York. Intrigued by rock gardens they had seen on their travels, Frank and Anne Cabot built several raised stone beds where they could grow alpine species and dwarf conifers. Before long they had added some greenhouses and started a modest nursery business, offering rock-garden species to other gardening enthusiasts.

An early problem these gardeners faced was the hilltop site's lack of water. They drilled wells and built a 20,000-gallon reservoir, hidden under a new pavilion, to pump water to a series of rivulets and pools. These have been developed into a pond garden on one side of the entrance drive and a rock pool on the other, bordered by plantings of rhododendrons and azaleas, as well as woodland gardens and the striking stream garden shown in the picture opposite.

Primroses, often used in areas of rock gardens that are shady or moist, come in a dazzling variety of color combinations like the two shown at right. A natural complement to rocks, flowers, shrubs, and trees is the element of water. Seen at far right is a stream garden and pool Frank Cabot built on the brow of a hill, overlooking a view of the Hudson Highlands in the distance.

The Middle Atlantic States

3

THE REGION of the middle Atlantic seaboard—New York, Pennsylvania, New Jersey, Delaware, Maryland, the District of Columbia, and Virginia—is a landscape of green, rolling hills; of farm fields and open meadows; of oaks, beeches, maples, dogwoods, and tulip trees. In the dappled shade of woodlands grow a variety of ferns, and wildflowers like trilliums, cranesbills, wild columbines, hepaticas, Virginia bluebells, and wild blue phlox. Wetter bottomlands sprout bright yellow marsh marigolds, red cardinal flowers, sweetflag, turtlehead, joe-pye weed, and pickerelweed. In summer, meadows glow with brilliant orange butterfly weeds, field daisies, sundrops, beebalm, black-eyed Susans, and chicory, and later with goldenrod and asters. Along the coast, bayberry and yarrow grow wild amid dune grasses.

To this native palette, gardeners add such perennial favorites as daffodils and tulips, peonies, lilies, phlox, foxglove, statice, irises, bleeding hearts, and forget-me-nots. Hostas are seen in many shady gardens, where pachysandra and periwinkle are widely planted as ground covers. In summer, annuals like impatiens, wax begonias, marigolds, petunias, and geraniums seem to be everywhere, and in autumn chrysanthemums abound. Roses are especially popular, as the number of fine rose gardens in the region attests.

The middle Atlantic states, indeed, are noted for their wealth of gardens of all kinds, both private and public, and for their many carefully tended public parks, whose oases of greenery offer respite from the pace of modern

Pink and lavender phlox and white foamflowers thrive in a wild garden in Pennsylvania.

life in cities like Philadelphia and Washington, D.C.

The Delaware Valley in particular, which has been described as "the gateway to America's gardens," boasts the largest concentration of arboretums and botanical gardens of any region in the United States. These gardens range in size and style from small, historic city plots, maintained by local horticultural societies, to world-renowned, once-private estates like Longwood and Winterthur, whose spacious grounds have been preserved and enhanced for everyone to enjoy.

In this region, gardening is a long-standing tradition, and one can trace its history here as perhaps nowhere else. Monticello, Mount Vernon, Williamsburg, and a score of other restored sites reveal the gracious and orderly patterns of eighteenth-century upperclass life. Gardens of the nineteenth century show the influence of the Victorian era and the romantic English landscape school. The great country estates built by wealthy industrialists in the early twentieth century illustrate a fascination for landscapes patterned after the styles of the gardens

of the French and Italian Renaissance.

An increasing number of mid-Atlantic gardens reflect contemporary ideas as well, including the use of water, native wildflowers, and ornamental grasses to achieve beauty, as well as practicality, in suburban and urban backyards.

Below: Shirley poppies and bachelor buttons brighten a Pennsylvania meadow. Right: old-fashioned hollyhocks adorn a Victorian seaside cottage in New Jersey. Far right: pink peonies, tulips, and lavender phlox, planted in a perennial border against a split-rail fence, frame a view of rolling farmland near Charlottesville, Virginia.

The rich yellow of goldenrod and the intense blue of New England asters (above) make a striking color contrast in a Brandywine Valley field. Left: orange butterflyweed, one of the most vivid of native wildflowers, attracts butterflies and admiring gardeners alike. Right: Virginia bluebells, with nodding clusters of pale blue, trumpet-shaped blossoms, create a spectacular forest show. A perennial that makes its appearance as early as March, the Virginia bluebell grows abundantly in moist woodlands throughout the mid-Atlantic region, and is a favorite in gardens, too.

Historic Homes and Country Places

PERHAPS no garden landscape in America more movingly evokes its time and place than Thomas Jefferson's Monticello. And no American was more the quintessential gardener than Jefferson himself. The lessons he learned firsthand about nature and plants, coupled with his talents as a designer, enabled him to create a work of landscape art that tens of thousands of visitors marvel at every year. Moreover, in many ways those lessons are as valid today—for other gardeners, in other times and places—as they were for Jefferson two centuries ago.

Jefferson had many pressing matters to attend to, but he always found time to return to his beloved "little mountain," to supervise the planting of new bulbs or saplings he had ordered from his favorite Philadelphia nursery, to scold his daughters for their inattention to the flowers, to sit and read in the large-windowed garden pavilion overlooking the Virginia hills.

His interest in gardens had little to do with fashion; it was rooted in the land. It sprang from an endless curiosity about the weather and its effects on crops, the life cycles of insects, native wildflowers and their blooming dates. He once remarked that there was "not a sprig of grass that shoots uninteresting to me."

In his *Garden Book* of daily chronicles and correspondence, Jefferson reveals the many possibilities of gardening. Along with music, poetry, sculpture, painting, architecture, and oratory, he considered gardening one of the seven "fine arts." A keen botanist and farmer, he sought out the best native plants, growing not only local species like the cardinal flower, Virginia bluebell, and wild columbine, but also Texas bluebonnet, Mandan corn, and Arikara beans brought back from the West by the expedition he commissioned of Lewis and Clark.

Jefferson was equally intrigued by what the rest of the world had to offer, in terms of both plants and design ideas. He prized the mimosa and goldenrain tree from China, grew thirty-six varieties of European grape and fifteen cultivars of his favorite vegetable, the English pea. While serving as Minister to France, he enthusiastically sent to Monticello seeds of the latest introductions, among them the garden heliotrope. ("A delicious flower," he noted. "The smell rewards the care.")

He also visited England and, admiring the new naturalistic landscap-

The West Lawn of Monticello was designed by Thomas Jefferson with a winding "roundabout" walk where guests could stroll to enjoy his changing flower displays.

ing that was becoming popular there, adapted to Monticello's contours its meandering lines and open, parklike vistas with trees set in groups. The 18-acre grove he created included not only a veritable arboretum of pet ornamental species but also a natural woodland area where existing native trees were thinned and trimmed up high, the scrubby undergrowth beneath them removed and replaced by a shining carpet of grass.

Making the most of the natural landscape—a notion that was to return to favor a century or more after his death—was in some ways Jefferson's ideal. "Gardens can be made without expense," he noted. "We have only to cut out the superabundant plants."

In a 1,000-foot-long vegetable garden, and a 400-tree orchard below it (both located on a south-facing hillside to catch the spring sun and avoid late frosts), he grew no less than 450 varieties of vegetables, herbs, fruits, and nuts, including the still-new tomato and eggplant, the Taliaferro apple ("the most juicy apple I have ever known"), and 37 cultivars of his favorite fruit, the peach.

Thomas Jefferson retired from public life in 1809—and quickly returned home to prepare new beds for a fresh shipment of hyacinths and tulips, whose bulbs had arrived labeled with fancy names. His granddaughter Ellen later recalled "running to Grandpa to announce that we really believed Mar-

cus Aurelius was coming up, or the Queen of Amazons was above ground! He would immediately go out and verify the fact, and praise us for our diligent watchfulness. Then, when the flowers were in bloom . . . how he would sympathize in our admiration, or discuss with my mother and elder sister new groupings and combinations and contrasts. Oh, these were happy moments for us and for him!" Like other gardeners, Grandpa Jefferson probably relished such moments most of all.

In The Grove at Monticello (below), Jefferson thinned a stand of native trees to show them at their best. At the edge of his long vegetable garden (right), he built a small pavilion.

From Far Hills to Charlottesville, the mid-Atlantic region is rich in gardens, old and new, large and small, many of which reflect the region's horticultural roots. Among these is a traditional love of flowers for their own sake, planted in beds and borders to create stunning tapestries of color, or to set off views of the verdant countryside beyond.

In formal gardens, borders are usually long and straight, and beds are laid out in rectangular or circular shapes.

In less formal designs, the beds assume freer outlines, with flowers planted in flowing drifts. The latter arrangement is well suited not only to many standard garden favorites but especially to wildflowers, which grow naturally that way. In some beds and borders, either formal or informal, flowers, shrubs and trees are mixed for contrasting effects, and further contrasted against an expanse of green lawn. Favorite flowers of mid-Atlantic gardeners include achillea, armeria, beebalm, campanula, candytuft, cleome, echinacea, forget-me-nots, lobelia, gaillardia, geraniums both hardy and tender, rudbeckia, sedum, pansies, marigolds, impatiens, zinnias, salvia, and veronica. Irises, astilbe, peonies, and roses are also popular in this part of the country.

A bright palette of azaleas and perennials enlivens a curving border in Virginia (above). Twin borders flank a formal stone walk (right), and a less formal path is planted with red and yellow tulips on the sides (far right).

Quite a different tradition is that of the "green garden," which relies largely on the evergreen colors of leaves and lawns for interest whether or not any flowers are in bloom. Some of these gardens emulate Colonial and English prototypes, using boxwood or yew as hedges that define formal outdoor rooms. The hedges are allowed either to billow naturally in rounded waves or are clipped into tailored, rectilinear forms, as they are in classic parterres (a concept that the Americans borrowed from the English, who appropriated it from the French, who were in turn inspired by ideas from the Italian Renaissance).

Here and there in a green garden one can see vestiges of the ancient art of topiary, the meticulous training and shearing of dense small-leaved trees and shrubs into geometric or fanciful shapes. A technique used to ornament the grounds of villas and palaces since Roman times, it was imported from England like many other horticultural ideas. Among those who liked it and could afford its upkeep, topiary enjoyed wide popularity in America, particularly in the mid–Atlantic region. Topiary was found both in early Colonial gardens in the region and on later country estates, but changing tastes and a desire among gardeners for low-maintenance plantings have made it far less appealing today. One of the few full-blown topiary gardens still in existence in this part of the country is on the Maryland estate of Harvey Ladew, a sculptor-gardener who delighted in shaping plants into all sorts of forms, from stately obelisks to a whimsical portrait of a hunter and his hounds.

Another approach taken in country gardens both large and small is to mix several kinds of plants—flowers, shrubs and trees, bulbs, and vines—in one bed or border. Sometimes these colorful plantings are contrasted against an expanse of green lawn. Mixed plantings can be seen in historic sites such as Williamsburg, great estate gardens like Dumbarton Oaks in Washington, D.C., and Winterthur in Delaware, and in private gardens throughout the region.

A newer, and undoubtedly more enduring tradition in the mid–Atlantic region, is the notion of a garden as a celebration of the native scene, a place where plants can be enjoyed as nature intended them to be.

At the Ladew Topiary Gardens in Monkton, Maryland, a hunter in pursuit of his hounds (below) contrasts with obelisks and fortresslike hedges framing a fountain pool (bottom right). Top right: tailored topiary at the William Paca House in Annapolis; (top, far right) billowing boxwood in a Virginia garden.

Perhaps the finest naturalistic gardens in the mid-Atlantic region—famous for spring displays of flowering shrubs, bulbs, and trees—are those of Winterthur, outside Wilmington, Delaware. The gardens were once part of the thousand-acre estate of Henry Francis Du Pont, who carefully preserved the essence of the natural countryside while introducing new species from around the world, often directing the placement of plantings himself. At left: a woodland aglow with Kaempferi azaleas and Spanish bluebells. Above: broad meadows at Winterthur adrift with daffodils.

Wildflower Gardens

GARDENING with native wild-flowers is becoming as popular in the middle Atlantic states as it is elsewhere, as many gardens in the region attest. Some of these gardens take woodland as their theme, using paths and underplantings of wildflowers to create pleasing pictures, but relying for their basic strength on the branching shapes and changing colors of the trees themselves. In open areas, other gardens capitalize on the grasses and flowers of natural meadows, with their constantly changing displays.

Among a number of organizations helping to further the popularity of native wildflowers is the Brandywine Conservancy River Museum in Chadds Ford, Pennsylvania, appropriately situated in a valley that is also celebrated both for its native landscapes and its native art. The conservancy's own wildflower gardens, extensive and colorful, surround a handsome nineteenth-century grist mill that was renovated to house the works of Andrew Wyeth, Jamie Wyeth, and other well-known artists of the Brandywine area. Started in the mid-1970s by volunteers, the gardens were designed to illustrate uses of plants native to the Brandywine region, as well as some that originated elsewhere but have become naturalized there.

Massed or mixed in informal beds and borders are striking displays of

The beauties of native wildflowers, seen here in late summer, are displayed in the gardens of the Brandywine Conservancy's River Museum in Pennsylvania. Far left: yellow tickseed sunflowers, named for their tenacious pronged seeds. Above: asters, goldenrod, and showy gaillardia, or Indian blanket, in beds.

black-eyed Susans, ox-eye daisies, goldenrod, sunflowers, sundrops, asters, blanketflowers, Canada lilies and Turk's-cap lilies, butterfly weed and joe-pye weed. In shady areas grow smaller woodland flowers like foamflowers, phloxes, violets, gentians, and bleeding hearts. Planted in sunny sweeps is the tawny day lily, a flower native to Europe and Asia that has been a favorite American species since Colonial days. Having managed to escape the confines of gardens and establish itself in the wild, this free-spreading day lily with its orange-red blossoms is now a familiar sight in summer along roadsides in the eastern United States.

All these wildflowers, besides being hardy and undemanding, are readily available and are easy to grow from seed. Like other organizations of its kind, the Brandywine Conservancy promotes conservation of native species by seed collection and propagation, and discourages the digging of plants from the wild that has despoiled many natural areas in recent years. Volunteers maintain the gardens, serve as guides, and propagate the wildflowers, both for use in the gardens and for sale in the museum shop.

Plantings at the Brandywine River Museum include showy masses of gaillardia (far left, top). Ox-eye daisies (bottom) were originally introduced from Europe but are now among the most familiar wildflowers of American roadsides and fields. Near left: a variety of rudbeckia, one of many members of the coneflower or black-eyed Susan family, blooms in fall against a barn.

Old-Fashioned Rose Gardens

THE ESTIMATED fifty million families who grow roses in this country are carrying on a proud tradition established by the first settlers. Rose gardening, in fact, dates back to much earlier times: wild roses are believed to have been the first ornamental plants brought into cultivation in China five thousand years ago. The rose, valued above all other flowers for its extravagant beauty, became the "Queen of Flowers" to the ancient Greeks. Developed by later hybridizers into myriad forms—there may be as many as fifteen thousand varieties today—it has been a favorite ever since, and nowhere more so than in the middle Atlantic states.

Rose gardens in the region take many shapes and sizes. There are city rose gardens and country rose gardens, of formal and informal design. Bush roses—hybrid teas, grandifloras, and floribundas—are often used in a border along a driveway, or sidewalk, or in an island bed surrounded by lawn. Climbing and rambling roses are trained to sprawl along fences, climb trellises, clamber over arbors. Shrub roses are often used as hedges. Gardeners pressed for space grow minia-ture roses in pots or small garden beds.

Roses can be demanding to grow—prone to attacks from Japanese beetles, mildew, and fungus diseases; needing careful fertilization and watering, and winter protection in cooler climes. But Americans love them nonetheless—enough to make the rose our official national flower. Dedicated rosarians learn how to get the most from their plants, using cultivars that bloom over long periods, or climbers and shrub roses that send up a second flush of bloom in fall.

To help gardeners choose among the many new rose cultivars that are constantly being introduced, All-America Rose Selections, an organization of rose breeders and nurserymen, maintains test gardens all over the country where volunteers try out new strains. Those that perform the best are awarded the coveted AARS seal.

In addition to the thousands of modern hybrids, gardeners are rediscovering the pleasures of growing old-fashioned, or heritage, roses, varieties that were in existence prior to 1867, when the first hybrid tea rose was introduced. Among these varieties are the intensely fragrant roses beloved of perfumers—damasks, moss roses, gallicas, bourbon roses. Old-fashioned

Beds of roses, peonies and foxgloves surround the statue of a young girl in a classic, old-fashioned garden in Princeton, New Jersey. Rose gardening is a horticultural endeavor with deep roots in the middle Atlantic states.

roses are becoming so popular among American gardeners, in fact, that a growing number of nurseries now specialize in them.

One of the earliest, and loveliest, gardens of old roses still in existence in this country is at Wyck, the oldest house in Philadelphia, situated in the section called Germantown. From the time it was built in the seventeenth century until it was opened to the public in 1973, Wyck was occupied by nine generations of the same Quaker family, all of them dedicated horticulturists. The present garden was designed in 1820 by a member of the family, Jane Bowne Haines, who planted some twenty varieties of roses available at the time—including the apothecary rose, the Scotch rose, and the Cinnamon rose, varieties known since 1500—and setting them off with borders of billowing green boxwood. Remarkably, many of these long-lived plants still come into bloom each spring after nearly 170 years.

Classic rose gardens in Philadelphia include the one at Wyck, the city's oldest house (near right and center right). Among venerable varieties displayed (above) are the apothecary rose and the red 'Rose de Rescht.' Top, right: the rose garden at the University of Pennsylvania's Morris Arboretum; below, right: 'Simplicity.'

Water Gardens

ALONG WITH plants, the oldest common denominator in gardens is water, used not only to keep things growing but as a decorative element in itself, a vital focus that delights the eye and soothes the soul. From ancient Egypt and Persia to India and the Orient, no garden was thought complete without water, whether it took the form of a fountain, a cascade, or a reflecting pool where waterlilies perfumed the air and brightly colored fish flashed in the depths.

While water gardens are increasingly popular in every region of this country, they are especially so in the environs of Maryland and Washington, D.C., where many homeowners grow waterlilies and other aquatic plants in backyard pools. Some of the pools are naturalistic, free-form shapes with stones placed around the edges. But since nature is not always easy to mimic convincingly, other owners have opted for frankly manmade geo-

In a small backyard pool in Mount Airy, Maryland (right), owners John and Noralie Katsu featured yellow tropical waterlilies in a landscaped setting, accented by a Japanese stone lantern. Far right: a larger pool in Maryland offers both swimming and a pleasant garden view, landscaped with grasses by Kurt Bluemel.

metric designs. Not a few are raised above ground within retaining walls—a solution that minimizes excavation; brings water and plants closer to the eye and easier to tend; allows sitting on the edges; and discourages debris, pets, and small children from winding up in the pool.

Favorite choices for planting are the many varieties of hardy and tropical waterlilies, whose blooms come in shades of white and yellow through red and purple, and the dramatic, richly scented lotus, which rises high above the water on 2- to 5-foot stems. Other decorative aquatic species include water poppy, floating heart, and water snowflake. For shallow edges and moist pool margins there are colorful water-loving irises, marsh mar-igolds, and cardinal flowers, as well as the striking foliage of arrowhead, pickerel rush, horsetails, dwarf papyrus, and bamboo.

On a Virginia estate (far left), yellow irises rise among other aquatic plants in a pool bordered by rocks and planted with azaleas and ferns to enhance its natural look. In a water garden in Potomac, Maryland (below), tropical waterlilies grow beside an Oriental-style bridge.

Graceful rabbit-ear irises, of a variety with distinctive, light-edged leaves (above), make a striking focal point in any water garden. At right: a handsome swimming pool nestled into a slope with stone retaining walls, and planted with graceful clumps of fountain grass.

Grass Gardens: Wild and Elegant

AS GARDENERS turn more and more to naturalistic gardens of native plants, the wildflowers of our fields and woodlands are playing featured roles. Rapidly rising stars, however, include the ornamental grasses, whose graceful shapes, still unfamiliar to many gardeners, stand out as elegant exclamation points.

Ornamental grasses have enjoyed special popularity in the mid-Atlantic region, where their use has been pi-oneered by landscape architects like Wolfgang Oehme and James van Sweden of the Washington firm of Oehme, van Sweden and Associates, and by Kurt Bluemel of Kurt Bluemel, Inc., nurserymen and landscape designers of Baldwin, Maryland, who offer many ornamental varieties as well as other decorative members of the grass family like sedges, rushes, and bamboos.

Relatives of the common lawn grasses that have long dominated the domestic landscape, the taller, unfettered ornamentals—some American natives but many of them deriving from Europe, South America, and the Orient—are beginning to take over from their close-cropped cousins, and for good reasons. They are beautiful almost year-round, sending up masses of slender green foliage and coming into bloom after other perennials to fill late gaps in the calendar of color. They provide interest even in winter with silvery seed plumes and stems of tan or gold that can also be cut and used in dried arrangements indoors. To add further interest to the garden year-round, ornamental grasses provide food, cover, and nesting spots for migrating and resident birds.

A variety of ornamental grasses animate gardens in the mid-Atlantic region designed by landscape architects Oehme, van Sweden & Associates. Distinctive for their tall, slender leaves and plumed heads, the grasses provide soft, billowing textures that add movement to the garden scene when they sway and rustle in the breeze, as well as lending a wonderful variety of color and form.

These grasses don't just sit there meekly underfoot—they look alive. Sparkling with dew or frost in the morning light, they wave and rustle in the wind, adding novel elements of motion and sound to the garden scene. They are also undemanding, requiring no special watering or fertilizing. Perhaps best of all, ornamental grasses don't have to be mowed. To keep the garden neat, all that is necessary is to cut and remove the older, brittle stalks in spring as new shoots rise to take their places.

In size and character, the grasses range from tiny blue fescues, whose clumps of steely blue shades seldom reach a foot in height, to giant pampas and plume grasses that can exceed twelve feet. Among the most beautiful in the middle range—and often used as garden accents—are maiden grass, Japanese silver grass, porcupine grass, zebra grass, and other members of the miscanthus group; the pennisetums, aptly named fountain grasses; and the bluestem grasses and panicums or switch grasses, which are American

natives. One of the most striking ornamentals—resembling a delicate upward explosion—is a variety called Karl Foerster's feather reed grass. It was named for a German nurseryman who fondly christened ornamental grasses "Mother Earth's hair."

A formal walled garden by Oehme, van Sweden (above) with plantings of tall grasses and yellow rudbeckias. Suburban landscapes by Kurt Bluemel are set off by fountain grass, Japanese blood grass, and the showy plumes of pampas grass (top, right); yellow foxtail grass and more Japanese blood grass (bottom, right).

Japanese silver grass, a variety of miscanthus with
white plumes, makes a stunning foil for the reds
of cardinal flower, eupatorium, and hibiscus (left).
The color of Japanese blood grass becomes more
intense in fall, providing striking accents in
November (above) and into winter's snows. The
whitish leaves of a miscanthus named 'Cabaret'
brighten a garden scene (right).

The Southeast

4

SOUTHERNERS have a special love for flowers. No wonder: They are blessed with an almost endless list of beautiful plants that flourish in the region's warm, moist air. The South is justly famous for its magnificent displays of azaleas and magnolias, often set against picturesque backdrops of spreading live oaks draped with Spanish moss. Equally cherished species are wisteria, jasmine, white Cherokee and yellow Banksia roses, many varieties of hollies, loquats with their huge clusters of pear-shaped yellow fruit, silverbells, snowbells, cherry laurels, and the fringe tree or "old man's beard." Showy, gorgeously colored Louisiana irises bloom in the cypress swamps in that state. Subtropical gardens in Florida are resplendent with exotic orchids, gingers, and heliconias.

The deciduous forests of the South-east are home to a wide array of plants including ferns, trout lilies, crested iris, Carolina allspice, flame azalea, wax myrtle, oakleaf hydrangea, honeysuckle, Virginia bluebells, Oconee bells, trilliums, and wild ginger. The flat coastal plains are characterized by long-needled pines with an understory of grasses. Wax myrtle and sweet bay magnolia grow here, and cypress trees thrive in the wetter areas. Carnivorous plants—pitcher plants and Venus flytraps—are also native to coastal plains.

Southern gardens take a variety of forms, the most elegant typified by broad, serene lawns, large old shade trees, and generous plantings of azaleas. Other classic plants of southern gardens are live oak, dogwood, English boxwood, jasmine, and liriope or

The classic South: an allée of native live oaks, underplanted with flowering azaleas.

lily-turf. In summer crape myrtles in their various shades of pink bloom in many backyards.

While some southern garden favorites are native plants, many more have been enthusiastically imported from abroad. The sweetly perfumed gardenia, a native of China, is named for one of Charleston, South Carolina's more notable early gardeners, a physician and gentleman botanist with the apt name of Alexander Garden. The poinsettia is named for another Charlestonian, Joel Poinsett, who discovered it while serving as the United States minister to Mexico and introduced it to the United States.

Perhaps the greatest contributions to southern horticulture, however, were made by a Frenchman, André Michaux, who established a nursery for native and imported species near Charleston in 1786. He is credited with introducing some of the region's best-loved plants, including the crape myrtle, Indian azalea, mimosa, tea olive, chinaberry, and ginkgo or maidenhair tree. Michaux's crowning achievement was the popularization of the common camellia, *Camellia japonica,* whose infinite varieties Southerners have treasured for more than two centuries.

Among the wealth of flowers found in the South, few can surpass the popularity of the camellia, one of whose hundreds of varieties is the pink beauty shown above. Other Oriental natives that have become thoroughly naturalized are the Cherokee rose (right), and the azalea, often displayed in massed banks of color (far right).

Spring and fall bring the most pleasant weather to the Southeast. Summer heat and humidity are often tough on gardens and gardeners alike. But mild winters make it possible for gardens to have flowers blooming all year. Camellias are a highlight in late autumn and winter, and cool-weather annuals and biennials such as larkspur and pansies bloom better in winter than summer. Tender perennials like snapdragons, which northerners must grow as annuals, can be treated as perennials in the South. In the warmest parts of the region, tender bulbs like cannas and gladiolus do not have to be unearthed and stored indoors over winter, but can stay in the ground all year. The fragrant paperwhite narcissus, which must be forced indoors in colder climates, can be grown outdoors in frost-free areas of the South.

From far left: jasmine and wisteria on garden gates in Charleston; variegated liriope, or lily-turf, in Mississippi; bougainvillea framing a formal garden scene in Miami.

Native Gardens

AZALEAS are more closely identified with the Southeast than perhaps any other plant. They are "big box-office" in this part of the country, as the crowds flocking to public gardens like Magnolia Plantation and Gardens and Middleton Place attest. They have become fixtures in private gardens, too. Indeed, azaleas are so omnipresent one might think they had been growing all over the region since the beginning of time.

Most of the azaleas on view in southern gardens, however, are not native species but showy modern hybrids, including introductions from England and Japan. Hybridizers have produced azaleas in every conceivable shade of red, rose, pink, and orange, along with white and numerous shades of purple, as well as cultivars adapted to different climate zones. While the massed colors and lavish blossoms of the hybrids tend to steal the show in both public and private gardens, people are coming to appreciate the special

. . . .

Vibrant pink azaleas, like these seen at Magnolia Gardens outside Charleston, South Carolina, are favorites of both residents and visitors in the Southeast. While many of the varieties commonly seen are modern hybrids imported from abroad, southerners are increasingly recognizing their own native species for special color and scent.

qualities of native species, not only azaleas but many other shrubs and wildflowers indigenous to the South.

At Callaway Gardens in Pine Mountain, Georgia, where more than 700 varieties of azaleas bloom, particular favorites are fifteen native species, which are sometimes called "honeysuckles" because many of them have a sweet scent. They are not only more fragrant than most hybrids, but are also hardier in winter, easier to care

for, and can look more natural in informal settings at home.

While the showy azaleas bloom mainly in April and May, the natives extend the show until fall. In March and early April, there are the Florida flame azalea, with its golden yellow flowers, and the Piedmont azalea, with blossoms ranging from white to deep pink. The orange Oconee azalea blooms in mid-April, followed by the orange-to-red flame azalea in June, and

the similar Cumberland azalea in late June to early July. A late-flowering form of the sweet azalea puts forth fragrant white blossoms in July and August. Callaway's proudest possession is the plum-leaved azalea, which

The delicate, light pink blossom of an azalea, glistening with raindrops in a garden in Avery Island, Louisiana (far left); a Kurume azalea named 'Hinodegiri,' photographed in Mississippi (near left), white and pink azaleas seen in a garden in Charleston, South Carolina (below).

grows naturally only within a radius of 100 miles. Its orange and red flowers, borne on branches that may reach 15 or 20 feet in height, light up the woodlands as late as September.

Many other native plants suitable to home landscapes are displayed at the North Carolina Botanical Garden in Chapel Hill, an institution dedicated to the conservation and propagation of plants of the Southeast. One garden features plants of the sandhills pied-mont, including long-leaf pine, turkey oak, loblolly bay, sweet bay, sand myrtle, and prickly pear. Another, devoted to the savannah of the coastal plain, has an outstanding collection of rare ground orchids and unusual, insect-eating bog species, including Venus flytraps, sundews, and pitcher plants. A mountain garden, especially appealing to some homeowners, shows off native mountain laurel, rosebay (from which the first garden rhododendrons were hybridized), and smaller woodland wildflowers like spring beauties, wild ginger, bluebells, and Oconee bells.

Rhododendrons and beebalm at the Atlanta Historical Society's Quarry Garden (above), which exhibits a wide range of species native to the Southeast. Another institution devoted to the region's rich flora is the North Carolina Botanical Garden at Chapel Hill, where wildflower plantings include blue-flowered Hyssop skullcap and orange butterflyweed (right).

Great Plantations

THE SPRAWLING plantations of the South were the foundations of the region's economy until the devastation of the Civil War. Today, few of these fine old estates produce tobacco, cotton, rice, or indigo as they used to, but many have taken on new life as historic and cultural sites. Each year hundreds of thousands of visitors tour their stately, columned mansions, wander over expansive lawns and through parklike groves of trees, admire the lavish plantings of formal gardens, stroll along allées framed by breathtaking displays of azaleas, camellias, and moss-draped oaks.

These are the classic southern gardens conceived on a grand scale by people who could afford them, and built, planted, and maintained by armies of slaves. The gardens most often contain masses of azaleas and rhododendrons, dogwood and magnolia trees, camellias, viburnum, and boxwood. Perennials grow in beds and borders, and pachysandra is widely used as a ground cover. The great plantations have cast a durable spell of romance, and they continue to influence garden design in the region more than any other single factor, both in plantings and architectural details.

. . . .

Scenes from South Carolina's Middleton Place. Far left: flower-bordered lagoons; an octagonal sunken garden with old tea-olive shrubs. Above: a close-up of the "azalea hillside," where thousands of plants bloom in a native woodland setting, above a dammed millpond.

Perhaps the finest example of the plantation style is Middleton Place, located upriver from Charleston, South Carolina. Now a 110-acre National Historic Landmark, it is recognized as the earliest major example of classical landscape design—and still one of the best—in the United States.

The gardens of Middleton Place were begun in 1741 when a twenty-four-year-old southern aristocrat named Henry Middleton began carving out of Carolina's Low Country wilderness a New World version of Versailles, a grand design of parterres, allées, and grassy terraces with a view of the Ashley River, framed by a pair of lakes in the shape of a butterfly's wings. The gardens were also something of a wedding present, for young Henry had recently married Mary Williams, a wealthy landowner's daughter who had brought to their union a handsome present of her own: the house and plantation they had just moved into and christened Middleton Place. Henry, who had developed a keen eye for landscape during travels in Europe, was determined to show his English relatives that their Colonial cousins, far from being country bumpkins, knew how to live in style.

What the Middletons and their descendants accomplished was not only a labor of love but a masterpiece. Middleton Place has been called the "premier garden of the thirteen colonies," and it remains a proud part of the gardening heritage of the South.

The central axis of Middleton Place sweeps from an entrance greensward (right) over grass terraces to lakes shaped like a butterfly's wings. The main house (below) faces out to a broad terrace.

Another outstanding, and quite different, example of the plantation style is Magnolia Plantation and Gardens, also located outside Charleston, not far from Middleton Place. The ancestral home of the Drayton family since the 1670s, and still owned and managed by a descendant, Drayton Hastie, Magnolia is regarded by many as the quintessential southern garden of beauty and romance.

"Brilliant with azaleas and magnolias, it centers around a pool of dreamy water overhung by tall trunks wanly festooned with the gray Florida moss," wrote the English playwright John Galsworthy on seeing the Magnolia Gardens more than a half century ago. "Beyond anything I have ever seen, it is otherworldly."

Dreamy and otherworldly though it is today, Magnolia was originally laid out in the formal style of a seventeenth-century English garden. In the early 1800s, John Grimke Drayton began to soften it along wilder, more naturalistic lines to create an "earthly paradise" that would make his Philadelphia-born wife Julia forget all ideas of returning North. Drayton is credited with introducing the first azaleas

Magnolia Plantation and Gardens outside Charleston are famed for darkly brooding lagoons that mirror stunning displays of flowering shrubs, set among the trunks and "knees" of huge bald cypress trees growing out of the water (far left). A much-photographed trademark of Magnolia Gardens is an old white bridge, seen at left, arching gracefully across one of the waterways.

to America—the *Azalea indica,* of which the gardens now boast some 250 strains. He was also among the first to use camellias as outdoor rather than indoor plants—no less than 900 varieties, 150 of them developed on the plantation itself, now bloom in an all-winter display. They are followed by an equally spectacular show of azaleas, tulips, and wisteria in spring, roses and annuals in summer, and chrysanthemums in fall, when the camellias start over again. At its peak, Magnolia is a veritable jungle of brilliant color, doubled by its own reflections in the dark waters of cypress lagoons—white dogwoods and pink chestnuts; yellow Banksia and white Cherokee roses; flowering cherries, peaches, and plums of every hue.

A conservationist as well as a gardener, Drayton Hastie has also updated the plantation's 500 acres into a wildlife refuge open to the public. Visitors can botanize or birdwatch on woodland walking trails, or paddle canoes through former rice fields along the river to observe myriad waterfowl.

One of the keys to Magnolia Gardens' popular success is its use of color—enough of it to awe even the most jaded visitor, as seen in massed purple irises (below), and the woodland walks ablaze with flowering shrubs (right).

Cities of Gardens

GARDENS in many southern cities—Charleston, Savannah, and New Orleans in particular—are well known for their Old World charm. In contrast with the expansive landscapes of their country cousins, and in keeping with European prototypes after which they were modeled, most of these gardens are small, enclosed by high walls for privacy, and laid out to provide a maximum of amenity in a minimum of space.

In a climate that can get oppressively hot, a typical city garden has at least one or two shade trees. It also relies on the psychologically cooling effect of dark green foliage, including ground covers of ivy and hedges of boxwood or privet, and often on the soothing splash of a small fountain in a basin or reflecting pool. Color and fragrance are equally treasured. Beds brim with annuals and perennials, supplementing seasonal shows of azaleas, dogwoods, camellias, and magnolias. Flowering vines like wisteria,

The Owens-Thomas house in Savannah (far left) is a re-creation of a formal 1820s garden, planted with boxwood, azaleas, Carolina cherry, and crape myrtle trees. At near left: the entrance to a private garden in Charleston, hidden from the street by vine-covered walls.

allamanda, and Confederate jasmine can be seen climbing trellises, twining around balconies, and spilling over garden walls everywhere.

Many of the gardens are geometrical or symmetrical in design; formal beds and borders are not only traditional in the region but fit in comfortably with older houses on rectangular lots, providing a sense of order and serenity. Such designs can make lovely visual patterns, particularly when viewed from the raised porches and second-floor balconies so characteristic of the South. Those porches and balconies—designed to provide shade and allow windows to be thrown open to cooling breezes—are also useful adjuncts to the garden scene. Not a few are enjoyed as garden spaces in themselves, with wicker furniture for relaxing, and containers of colorful flowers placed behind a lacy railing of wrought iron to welcome passersby on the street.

Among the city gardens of the South, those of downtown Charleston have few equals for beauty, variety, and old-fashioned charm. Concentrated in the old part of the city on the peninsula between the Ashley and Cooper rivers, these gardens and the historic houses they grace—many dating back to the early 1800s and before—draw waves of appreciative visitors each year.

Some of the gardens are large and formal, some small and informal, but all reveal a traditional love of plants and a scrupulous attention to detail. In a city noted for its good manners, even functional driveways and side alleys combine hospitality with pride. Framed by graceful wrought-iron gates, paved in patterned brick and stone, they are planted as miniature gardens in their own right to lend a note of welcome.

A hallmark of Charleston homes and gardens is the fine sensitivity with which pathways and plantings are set off by ornamental wrought-iron details. These touches range from graceful stair railings and filigreed entrance gates (below) to urn-topped garden columns and freestanding arches decorated with floral motifs (right).

Rivaling Charleston in European charm is Savannah, Georgia, a gentle city celebrated for its public squares—a score of shady, gardenlike oases that punctuate downtown in a green, rhythmic pattern, slowing traffic to a civilized pace and glorifying the urban scene. Stroll about, however, and you soon become aware of something else: Savannah's passion for gardens radiates to virtually every private front stoop, side alley, and backyard as well.

Here, behind wrought-iron filigree and pierced brick walls that let welcome breezes through, are the city's hidden horticultural gems. Some are lavish parterres with fountains, statuary, and clipped boxwood beds.

Others are closer to postage-stamp-size, modern versions of ancient walled gardens with barely enough room for some chairs, a table, and a few pots of geraniums under a flowering dogwood tree. In all of them, however, one is struck by a love of flowering color, and of fragrance. Even a single tea olive can perfume an entire garden when it is in bloom.

Yellow jasmine cascades over an ancient brick wall in Charleston (far left), sharing some of the beauty of a private garden with passersby on the street. Focal points in many gardens are bits of sculpture (left), often combined with fountains. Their crowning glories, however, are canopies of flowering trees like the one above, seen against a contrasting backdrop of purple wisteria.

Tropical Fantasies

T HE PURSUIT of paradise on earth is perhaps nowhere so dramatic as in Florida, where gardens frequently summon up images of Eden or the primeval jungle, depending on one's point of view. Lush, verdant, luxuriant, exuberant, exotic—these are the words people use to describe them. And, by and large, they are right.

The climate of southern Florida is much like that of the Mediterranean area—particularly Spain and Italy— and the influence of these countries is seen in the architecture and gardens of the region. Some large estates were patterned on Italian Renaissance styles; an outstanding example is Villa Vizcaya in Miami, originally built for an International Harvester heir. The grand formal gardens of these vast homes echo the Italian flavor of the buildings. More common sights in south Florida, though, are architecture and garden features derived from Spanish styles. White stucco walls, wide verandas, red tile roofs, and shady courtyards show the unmistakable influence of the Spaniards who first colonized the area.

Plantings by landscape architect Raymond Jungles enliven the entrance to a Florida home (far left), and an interior court (left).

In the hot, steamy climate of south Florida, plants grow quickly and in spectacular profusion, not only native species but a wide range from other subtropical regions of the world. Gardens here are full of banyans, bamboos, bananas, breadfruits, bird-of-paradise plants, and, of course, the familiar, waving palms. Countless varieties of orchids, the most extravagantly gorgeous of flowering plants, are seen in pots and hanging baskets on display on balconies and porches everywhere.

If there is such a thing as a typical Florida garden—a matter open to dispute in any region—it would be one in which the harsh sun and burning heat of summer are tempered by large, dark green, glossy leaves that cast cool patterns of dappled light. The dark greens of many tropical plants are also psychologically cooling, notes a leading Miami landscape architect with the apt name of Raymond Jungles; in this climate gardens that contain only bright greens can feel too sunny and

hot. In addition, he points out, the big, bold leaves of many such plants, when densely clustered, give a natural "jungle" look and help reduce maintenance, because people don't feel they have to prune the plants all the time.

. . . .
A garden of bromeliads thrives in the shade near an old Florida home (above, left). White orchids and lavender wisteria frame the windows of another house (above, right). Balconies in the South are often decked with climbing vines (top, right), and walled gardens provide cool retreats from the blazing sun (bottom right).

Bold, dark foliage also makes a fine contrasting backdrop against which to display the brilliant colors of many tropical flowers—the reds and magentas of bougainvilleas and Hong Kong orchid blossoms, the pinks and scarlets of bromeliads, the golds and crimsons of gingers and heliconias, as well as the vivid hues of seasonal flowers like impatiens, begonias, and geraniums. All of these also show to advantage against the whites and pastels of Florida house and garden walls.

As in other regions that are hot, Floridians welcome water as both a cooling and a colorful element in their gardens, whether it is the alluring sparkle of a turquoise swimming pool on a sunny patio or the splash of a small cascade in a dark woodland glen rimmed with the bold shapes of philodendrons, the spiky leaves of bromeliads, and the delicate fronds of ferns.

. . . .

At the Marie Selby Botanical Gardens in Sarasota, Florida, a waterfall cascades into a pool of flowering waterlilies surrounded by a jungle of philodendrons, gingers, and other tropical plants (far left). Also at Selby are orchids, heliconias, and bromeliads (below, left), the latter including red- and yellow-flowering aechmeas (right).

The Midwest

5

THE HEARTLAND of America encompasses a variety of landscapes, from the rolling woodlands of Ohio to the plains of Nebraska to the soaring Rocky Mountains of Idaho. The Rockies, of course, boast the country's most breathtaking scenery—relatively young, still-jagged peaks of naked stone, clothed at lower elevations by the tall, dark spires of spruces and firs. Rocky Mountain wildflowers are also among the most spectacular to be found, brightening the forests and splashing the upland meadows with color from spring to fall. Both these mountains and their plants are having an increasing impact on the region's garden styles.

Perhaps the most distinctive aspect of the Midwest, however, is the central Great Plains, the vast prairie of grasses and wildflowers that once stretched toward the horizon under an endless blue sky. Today almost all of that prairie has disappeared under farms, and, more recently, housing developments, fast-food chains, and discount stores. But a growing number of midwesterners have belatedly recognized its value as a symbol of their natural heritage, and have set aside some of the remaining patches in public prairie preserves.

Recognizing both the beauty and practicality of native grasses and wildflowers that tolerate drought, require no fertilizers, and need rough mowing only once or twice a year, state highway departments are using them on roadsides and embankments in preference to finicky, high-maintenance lawn grasses. Many corporations and institutions are joining this trend for

An Illinois meadow blossoms with milkweed, black-eyed Susans, and Queen Anne's lace.

their own landscaping needs. Prairies, as well as natural woodlands, are also becoming popular themes on a smaller scale: more and more gardeners are turning to native landscaping in their own backyards.

Despite urbanization, the Midwest is still farm country at heart; the tradition of growing one's food has been carried on quite naturally, and proudly, since pioneer days, when it was a necessity for everyone. While home gardeners enjoy growing their own vegetables all across the nation, a higher percentage continue to do so in the central states. Here the vegetable garden is as much a part of the vernacular as the grain silo and the cattle barn, though modern gardeners have learned to do the old things in some imaginative new ways.

Above: sunflowers frame a windmill on a farm in the Sandhills of Nebraska. Right, top: prairie blazingstars rise like bright pink rockets above a Nature Conservancy preserve on the Konza Prairie in Kansas. Right, bottom and far right: scenes of wildflower meadows in Michigan.

Above: Queen Anne's lace, a tap-rooted ancestor of the garden carrot, stretches toward the horizon; its fine, flat-topped flower clusters form a sea of white. A biennial plant native to Europe, it has spread aggressively to fields and road-sides all over the United States. At right: goldenrod and prairie blazingstars lend late summer color to a meadow in Illinois.

Native Landscapes

AMONG THE earliest and most influential champions of native landscaping was Jens Jensen, a nature-loving Dane who settled in Chicago in the 1880s, working first as a laborer in the public park system and later as a designer of both parks and gardens of private homes.

Like his friend and occasional collaborator Frank Lloyd Wright—celebrated promoter of the horizontal,

ground-hugging "prairie style" in architecture—Jensen took inspiration from the prairies and woodlands of the Midwest, advocating them as the most appropriate expression of the region's landscape, as well as a symbol of rebellion against the pretentiousness of the times. As Leonard K. Eaton wrote in his book about Jensen, *The Landscape Artist in America:*

> [He] scorned the eastern landscape architects who designed formal Italianate gardens around New York, Philadelphia, and Boston. They were, he thought, simply repeating the outmoded forms of Europe. Even worse, they were bringing the artistic manifestations

of political absolutism to a democratic republic where these forms had no place. For Jensen the allée, the parterre, and the grand boulevard were identified with autocratic government. The prairie, on the other hand, was a symbol of freedom and opportunity.

While du Ponts and Deerings opted for Italian or French Renaissance gardens in their estates outside Philadel-

At the Lincoln Memorial Garden in Springfield, Illinois, Jens Jensen and garden club volunteers transformed 77 acres of bare fields into a living showcase of plants native to Abe Lincoln's state. Below: a wildflower meadow. At right: a dogwood-bordered path beckons walkers as it disappears around a bend.

phia and Miami, Jensen managed to persuade a host of wealthy midwestern clients—Fords, Armours, Cudahys, Ryersons—of the simplicity and soundness of his newfound "American" ideas. He sometimes had to fight to discourage them from spending money purely for show, and he could be formidable in defense of his beliefs. When one client told Jensen he wanted to build a French chateau in the fashionable Chicago suburb of Lake Forest, Jensen growled, "You are an American. Why do you want to be a stuffed shirt?"

Jensen's designs did not seek to impress others with their owners' importance. Nor did they subscribe to the "romantic" or "picturesque" school, whose preconceived, often arbitrary simulation of nature had become a fashionable style in itself. He sought, rather, to express the true spirit of the native landscape and the beauty of native plants, growing in the kinds of places and associations in which they were found in the wild—an approach that gave his results not only a free and natural sweep, but a feeling of friendliness and repose. To Jensen, the greatest compliment was that a landscape of his "must have always looked this way."

The simplicity and strength of Jens Jensen's designs can be seen in some of his few remaining landscapes. Far left: a grove of native trees. Left, above: a rustic wooden bridge. Left, below: a stone path leading through a woodland.

One of Jensen's trademarks is a painterly use of light and shadow that makes the most of the sun at different times of the day; another is a sensitive molding of outdoor spaces into flowing sequences of different sizes and shapes. Open meadows—deliberate echoes of the prairie—are employed as major vistas, and are often oriented to provide views of the rising or setting sun, which he felt were among the many rhythms of nature from which people had become too far removed. At the edge of a meadow, as a transition between it and taller forest, he would place a margin of smaller native trees, such as hawthorns, to emphasize the perspective with their horizontal branches. A favorite trick—used to good effect even in modest gardens today—was to place irregularly shaped garden beds and clumps of plantings so that the lawn in which they were set curved in a dog-leg around them and mysteriously out of sight, making the area seem much larger than it was.

Always the intent was to draw the observer out into the landscape, to make him want to wander through it and enjoy it as it changed from hour to hour, from day to day, and from season to season through the year. Not many of Jensen's works survive, but those parks and gardens that do, fulfill this intent, and testify to Jensen's ultimate goal: "to bring to the city dweller a message of the country outside his city walls."

A characteristic of Jensen's work is his masterful placement of trees, seen above bordering a parklike meadow on a Ford family estate. At right are other Jensen trademarks; a curved stone bench forming a "council ring"; a rugged stone footbridge spanning a small creek; a flight of stone steps leading up a quiet hillside.

Prairie Gardens

THE IDEA of landscaping with native plants has taken root in a "prairie garden" movement that is spreading through more and more midwestern communities. Because prairie wildflowers and grasses are native to this part of the country, they are, first of all, appropriate. They are also relatively easy to maintain. The plants naturally tolerate the cold winters and hot, dry summers without needing watering or winter protection.

Prairie plantings are colorful, too. The midwestern wildflower palette includes such beauties as bright orange butterfly weed; rich golden tickseed, black-eyed Susan, and goldenrod; soft yellow evening primrose; yellow-and-red Indian blanket; brilliant red cardinal flower; scarlet Indian paintbrush and gilia; pinkish lavender purple coneflower; rosy purple liatris; purple asters; pink wild onion; blue false indigo, lewis flax, and camassia; white Queen Anne's lace; and penstemons in shades of pink, red, and blue.

Black-eyed Susans, members of the sunflower family, brighten a field in summer. This biennial species, native to the prairie, blooms from June through October across the United States. It is a special favorite of midwesterners, who often use it in their gardens.

One city with a dedicated group of prairie gardeners is Milwaukee, Wisconsin. Gardener Lorrie Otto, their leader, has been an eloquent champion of no-mow "meadow" gardening for more than a dozen years. Otto and more than a hundred of her neighbors are members of what they call the Wild Ones Natural Landscaping Club. The Wild Ones not only swap ideas and seeds; they sponsor annual tours of members' gardens every year in late July or early August, teaching other interested homeowners how to put away their lawnmowers and live with the more colorful and varied world of native plants.

While some communities insist on front-yard conformity—not a few have "weed ordinances" that can land the adventurous in court—Lorrie Otto and her friends find that they make far more converts than enemies. "People ask if they can walk through the paths and enjoy the gardens," she says by way of explanation. "It's just too pretty for complaints."

Otto's own yard is all garden, no lawn. Because it is located in a region where the western prairie and the eastern forest meet, half an acre is a prairie meadow and the other half-acre is planted in woodland wildflowers, trees, and shrubs. In early spring the woodland area comes alive with bloodroot, wild geraniums, violets,

trilliums, hepaticas, and anemones. In late spring and summer, irises, wild roses, and sunflowers burst into bloom in the meadow garden, and butterflies alight on the big lavender flower heads of joe-pye weed. By September the meadow glows with the whites of yarrow and boneset, the purples of asters, and the rich, mustardy yellows of goldenrod. Even after the colors of autumn have faded, birds continue to animate the garden, seeking out the tall

In Lorrie Otto's Milwaukee garden, a path is lined with wild strawberries, wild geraniums, violets, and buttercups (below). Otto and her neighbors use many native species in their yards, including prairie coneflowers (right, below) and greenheaded coneflowers, (far right, below).

seedheads of coneflowers and black-eyed Susans, which sketch their own graceful patterns against the snow. Lorrie Otto feels sorry for neighbors whose conventional lawns look bleak, particularly at this time of year.

Other enthusiasts of native landscapes, like Otto, point out that gardening with native wildflowers and grasses is economical, too. Ron Bowen, a prairie garden designer in Minnesota, has calculated that prairie-type planting costs roughly half as much per acre to install as turf grass, and as little as one-ninth as much in annual maintenance.

Many seed companies now offer an assortment of brightly packaged wild-flower mixes, many of them tailored to specific regions and environments to improve chances of success. While the notion of a "meadow in a can" is appealing, however, one doesn't simply stop mowing the lawn, sprinkle some seeds on the ground, and stand back to watch the show. A wildflower garden, like any other, requires soil preparation, planting, watering, and weeding until it has become established, which may take two or three years. But, once established, its plants, quite used to local climate and rainfall, thrive without fertilizing, watering, or applications of chemicals for weeds and pests. Little care is required save for cutting back the plants once a year and pulling up unwanted weeds and tree seedlings as they appear.

Nevertheless, to gardeners who grow native plants, the payoff comes not so much in less work but in greater satisfaction, a chance to enjoy a back-yard window on the changing natural world. There is also a feeling of identity. "My plants say midwestern America," says Lorrie Otto. "They give me a sense of place."

In Bayside, Wisconsin (left), environmental designer Donald Vorpahl helped Stephen and Rae Sweet convert an ordinary front lawn into a colorful, low-maintenance prairie garden of native grasses and flowering plants. Below: wildflowers grown from a "Heart of Idaho" mix at High Altitude Gardens in Ketchum.

American Ingenuity

EXPERIMENTING with a variety of styles and ideas can lead to a garden that breaks familiar rules, emerging as a unique expression of its owners and their particular plot of land. The result can be the most "American" style of all, a celebration of individual ingenuity.

Such a garden is that of Balthazar and Monica Korab, who thirty years ago bought an old farmhouse and four acres of run-down, overgrown land in Troy, Michigan, outside Detroit. Over the years they cleared out the brush, adding plantings and other touches as the spirit moved them.

"It just sort of happened. It's an immigrant's garden, a junk collector's garden," says Balthazar, who was born in Budapest and practiced architecture in Detroit before becoming a renowned photographer. Along the way, the garden has become a world of almost daily discoveries for its owners, who enjoy it in all its changing seasons, moods, and lights, Balthazar capturing each faithfully on film. It is a garden that is eclectic yet

Focal points in the Korab's garden (above) include a small pool with irises and decorative stones, and a field of poppies.

original, intensely personal—a landscape of the mind's eye.

The old farmer's lilacs are still there, now emphasized as a sculptural group with branches pruned upward to reveal gracefully twisting trunks. The big silver maples are there, too—a hollow in one occupied by a raccoon family that on summer evenings is sometimes seen peering comically at guests on the terrace below. Part of the property is kept in meadow, with clumps of bright poppies planted to frame the wheels of an old horse-drawn farm machine. The meadow was a wild sea of Queen Anne's lace until the town ruled that it had to be mowed lest "weed seeds" spread to contaminate the lawns of new housing developments across the road.

In a sumac meadow behind the house, the Korabs made a handsome sculptural group out of salvaged telephone-cable spools.

*The Korabs' back lawn, seen from the iris pool (above), leads up to a mound
where Balthazar transformed old barn timbers into sculptures, which he could
see from his bedroom window (when the tallest fell down, he simply
incorporated it into a new composition). In a court outside the kitchen (right),
the Korabs enjoy a colorful bower of hanging plants and climbing vines.*

Within their private domain, screened from creeping suburbia by old hedgerows and new white pines, the Korabs delight in flowers, planting new varieties that catch their fancy from time to time. The little courtyard outside the kitchen, trellised with wisteria and clematis vines, is crammed with an exuberance of potted geraniums, petunias, impatiens, and ferns—some planted imaginatively in the pedestals of old wash basins salvaged from the remodeled house. Irises surround a small pool nearby, which is ornamented with beautifully rounded, striated stones found on the shore of Lake Superior, and a perennial border full of colorful lilies curves up the slope to a homemade stone wall in back. Another garden, laid out between the house and an old barn used as a photographic studio, features the tall accents of arborvitaes and the feathery plumes of astilbes, underplanted with masses of spring-blooming trilliums native to the Michigan woods, a natural landscape whose relentless disappearance the Korabs mourn.

"A garden is not a product; it's a process," Balthazar Korab observes. "That's half the fun. It can be hard work, too. But it's a labor of love."

While clearing out underbrush from the old farm they bought, the Korabs saved some ancient lilacs, (far left). The perennial garden (left) is Monica Korab's special domain. Her husband recalls one day when he cut a few flowers to frame a picture he was taking. "When she found out," he says, "she bought $500 worth of lilies in revenge."

Edible Landscapes

CLOSE TO thirty million households—one of every three in America—grow their own vegetables and fruits, according to the National Gardening Association of Burlington, Vermont. Roughly a third of these households are in the Midwest. This oldest, most basic type of garden is still alive and well it seems, though in recent decades vegetable gardening has taken on some new and intriguing twists.

While raising one's own food was once a necessity, and still is done to save money, people do it today for largely different reasons. The primary one is the simple fact that fresh, home-grown produce tastes so much better than tired supermarket fare, which may have traveled many days and hundreds of miles before reaching the store. Many gardeners find, too, that the growing provides its own rewards, including the satisfaction of getting one's hands into the soil on a bright spring day, and the joy of watching a

Vegetables can be nice to look at as well as eat. In the prize-winning garden of Brenda Olcott-Reid in Chetopa, Kansas (far left), corn shares the spotlight with the blossoms of cosmos. Robert Kourik showcases vegetables in raised beds in this California garden shown at left.

tiny seedling gradually emerge from the earth, eventually producing a juicy red tomato that can be eaten right off the vine still warm from the sun. In these days of ecological awareness, not a few gardeners also cite respect for the environment as well as personal health, preferring a natural product they can control to one that has been readied for market with heavy applications of chemical fertilizers and pesticides. Finally, growing one's own vegetables allows the gardener to enjoy unusual varieties that may be hard to find in local markets.

The edible landscape has changed in other ways in recent years. Growing methods have been elaborated with new techniques and tools, from pre-packaged seed-starting kits to plastic mulches and protective seedling tents. Seed companies offer a number of choices, including "gourmet" vegetables from Europe and China, newly developed miniature strains that can be grown in pots on apartment balconies, and mouth-watering old-fashioned "heirloom" varieties that were almost lost in the hybridizers' rush toward bigness and uniformity but that have now been revived.

Another change in the way midwesterners—and gardeners everywhere—regard the food garden is the growing realization that many vegetables and fruits are not only good to eat but are also good to look at, that they don't have to be hidden away somewhere in the backyard by themselves. Purple-leaved basils, red-stemmed varieties of Swiss chard, scarlet runner beans with their rich red flowers are among the varieties that can be interesting to the eye as well as to the taste buds. When growing vegetables are imaginatively arranged in the home landscape and combined with flowers, their ornamental qualities can be brought out to lend a fresh and unexpectedly colorful dimension to garden design.

A traditional love of neatness is seen in the patterned rows of a vegetable garden in Roscoe Village, a reconstructed nineteenth-century town in Coshocton, Ohio (below). At right: broccoli and wildflowers, in trial beds at High Altitude Gardens, a seed nursery in Ketchum, Idaho.

Rocky Mountain Gardens

WHILE the scenery is stunning, the climate of the Rocky Mountains is drier than one might expect; in some places rainfall is so sparse that conditions are almost desertlike. Gardeners adapt by planting drought-tolerant alpine, prairie, and desert species, including a variety of wildflowers and other native plants.

Among the many lovely woodland wildflowers of the region is the Rocky Mountain columbine, Colorado's state flower, whose blossoms are rich violet-blue with white centers. In open areas grow other natives—camassia, Indian paintbrush, gay-feather, penstemons, lewis flax—that tolerate hot weather and dry soil. Where the soil is moist, in low-lying meadows and next to streams, the Rocky Mountain iris blooms in spring. Well adapted, too, to local conditions are trees like aspen, ponderosa pine, and Douglas fir, and, at higher elevations, limber pine, spruces, and firs.

On a hillside near Sun Valley, Idaho, Florence Mulder designed her garden (right and far right) with native species for drought tolerance and low maintenance. Working with Bill McDorman of High Altitude Gardens as consultant, she planted a variety of red, lavender, and yellow penstemons, yellow coreopsis, red coral bells, scarlet gilia, and feathery pink prairie smoke.

An extraordinary series of gardens that capture the spirit of the mountains surround Vickridge, a hilltop hacienda south of Denver, where the plains of the Midwest meet the towering ramparts of the Rocky Mountain Front.

The house, like its gardens, makes the most of its setting, its dramatic shapes of rounded stucco and angular stone suggesting both ancient Indian pueblos and the rugged building blocks of the mountains themselves. Freestanding walls, originally designed to descend the slope in rigid steps, were left unfinished on top to recall the ruin of a pueblo not far away. Rising in a rough U-shape, the walls enclose a lushly landscaped entrance court on the east where, sheltered from mountain winds, guests are greeted by a fountain and reflecting pool made of massive blocks of stone. Windows sweep around other sides of the house to open up views of the plains, and of Devil's Head Mountain to the west and Pike's Peak to the southwest.

Among the most dramatic features of Vickridge are the terraces, pools, and plantings that cascade down the slope, echoing those of hillside villas on the Mediterranean (which the owners also admire). Also built of stone, they are planted with a wide range of ornamental species, including colorful mountain varieties like saxifrages, thyme, dianthus, and low-growing phlox. The landscape around the house and gardens was carefully preserved in its original condition, with scrub oaks and ponderosa pines framing the views and native wildflowers and grasses growing right up to the walls.

. . . .

Views of Vickridge, a private home on a Colorado hilltop, reflect the beauty of the region's wildflowers. The house, designed by Ford, Powell & Carson and Lake/Flato Architects, was landscaped by Todd Bennitt.

The Southwest

6

PAINTERS and photographers have long been fascinated by the American Southwest, whose dramatic landscapes are unlike any others—angular compositions sculpted out of rock, sand, cactus, and mesquite, brilliantly lit by the changing colors of the desert sky.

Many areas of the Southwest are indeed desert, with blazing sun, harsh winds, poor soils, and rainfall amounting to only 10 or 12 inches a year, a fraction of what other areas of the United States are accustomed to. The critical factor for supporting both animal and plant life in the Southwest is water, a costly commodity that many communities have found it necessary to ration, particularly when it comes to the maintenance of lawns and garden beds.

Despite the low rainfall, however, the desert does not lack color. Foliage ranges from soft silvery grays to bright yellows and deep, rich greens. The region boasts a brilliant palette of wildflowers that burst into bloom in spring, after the winter rains. Among the most beautiful are those of the cacti, which blossom extravagantly among their formidable spines.

In addition to the tall saguaro cacti that stand like sentinels on the sandy wastes, several other kinds of cactus grow wild. There are squat, fiercely spined hedgehog and barrel cacti; prickly pears with their broad, flat pads; the tall, bizarrely twisted organ-pipe cactus; fine-spined pincushion cacti, and others. Their smooth-petaled flowers, many of them large,

Native California poppies blanketing the rolling hills of a southwestern desert.

(1 6 5)

some satiny or diaphanous, appear in brilliant shades of yellow, pink, magenta, and red.

Desert wildflowers include tickseed, lupine, devil's claw, desert marigold, datura, penstemon, chia, hummingbird trumpet, and zephyr lily. When the earliest wildflowers bloom in spring, especially after a wet winter, the deserts of the Southwest are magically transformed into seas of waving greenery dotted with color. It is an extraordinary sight. The wildflowers

are followed by the lavish cactus blossoms, but all too soon the heat of late spring sets in, and by summer the desert is dry and barren once again, with only the cacti and shrubs like ocotillo, creosote bush, and jojoba standing on the flat expanses of sand and rocks.

The desert, though characteristic of the region, is by no means the only landscape of the Southwest. Shrubby areas of chaparral are home to small trees and shrubs like madrone, manzanita, ceanothus and evergreen oak,

and to wildflowers like clarkia, checker lily, and matilija poppy. At cooler elevations there are woodlands of pinyon pines and junipers, along with serviceberry, wild zinnias, and canyon phlox. In high mountain areas grow

The protective spines of Teddy-bear cholla, a species of opuntia cactus, give plants a deceptively soft look as they catch the desert sun (below). Among myriad wildflowers native to the Southwest (right) are orange-yellow poppies, the peach-colored blooms of an echinopsis cactus, the yellow blossoms of prickly pear.

aspens, Douglas firs, ponderosa pines, and a variety of wildflowers like pasqueflower and lewisia. Texas alone has an almost incredible diversity of habitats, from deserts and forests to beaches and wetlands along the Gulf Coast, each with its own distinctive and colorful community of plants.

Gardens in the Southwest are as varied as the region's untamed landscapes. Because summers are so intensely hot and dry, much gardening is done during the winter. Gardeners grow annuals in winter and spring, and plant vegetable gardens in fall and winter. Gardens of cacti and other native plants are increasing in popularity because they are naturally suited to the climate and require far less maintenance than other kinds of gardens. Many gardeners temper the microclimate in their gardens by incorporating shade and water into the design. Spanish and Moorish influences turn up in courtyard gardens throughout the region. Swimming pools, too, are part of many home landscapes—oases of cool blue water that help homeowners withstand the desert heat.

Some newcomers to the Southwest fail to appreciate, at first, the horticultural diversity that the region has to offer and how greatly the climate here differs from the climate back East. They try to bring their eastern-style gardens with them, struggling to maintain the familiar lawns and flowers they remember from Ohio or New York. Alas, gardens of roses or pe-

rennials do not grow readily in the hot, arid conditions. Extraordinary quantities of water are required to maintain these plants and even if they get it, they do not perform as they do in more hospitable climes. Only gradually does the transplanted southwestern gardener realize that other kinds of gardens are better suited to this region, from both a practical and an aesthetic point of view.

More experienced southwesterners long ago discovered the virtues of using native plants, which are far better adapted to the climate—tough, drought-resistant species that require little care. Many of these plants also provide the raw material for the region's own bold and special kind of landscape art. Agaves, or century plants, seem to spout from the sand like frozen fountains, their huge, bluish or gray-green leaves describing incredibly graceful, tapering curves. The swordlike leaves of yuccas make explosive accents, while the tall columns of saguaro cacti provide dramatic counterpoints to low flat roofs, their impact doubled by their shadows etched by the sunlight on the sand.

The desert's dry and rocky landscape is home to many plants that long ago adapted to its harsh conditions. This scene in southwestern Arizona shows several of the region's trademarks: the giant saguaro cactus, whose candelabra-shaped trunks can eventually grow 50 feet tall and 2 feet thick; the ocotillo, whose thorny, whiplike stems are tipped with red flowers in spring; and lower-growing flowers like owl clover and bladderpod.

Going Native

"I T'S A REAL challenge to garden in the desert," says Judy Mielke, senior horticulturist at the Desert Botanical Garden in Phoenix, Arizona. "Heat, intense sunlight, drying winds, and winter cold take their toll on all but the hardiest of plants. Anyone looking for species that can stand up to those conditions should look first to the natives. Over thousands of years they have evolved ways to stay the course."

To deal with lack of moisture, many desert plants have shallow, spreading root systems that are near enough to the surface to take advantage of even the lightest rains. Other water-conserving features are the thick barrel or paddle shapes of cacti, which act as storage tanks, and the waxy skins or tiny, fuzzy hairs that insulate the leaves of many other succulents. Some trees and shrubs, like the paloverde and ocotillo, go even further: they actually drop their leaves during severe droughts so moisture cannot be transpired, then grow new leaves when water becomes available again.

The distinctive shapes of a tall ocotillo, contrasted with a low clump of paddle-shaped cacti, set off the arched entrance in an Arizona home (left). Among the most beautiful of the trees native to the region, and a special favorite of gardeners, is the blue paloverde (above), whose blue-green branches bear feathery cascades of bluish leaves.

Knowledgable gardeners in the Southwest make extensive use of drought-tolerant native trees, shrubs, and wildflowers, setting off their shapes and colors against neutral backgrounds of light-hued gravel or desert sand, as in the landscape above, which is centered on the blue-green leaves of an agave. At right: a variety of cacti and other species are arranged as a striking introduction to the modern Arizona home of Mike and Helen Greenberg. The plantings were designed by Steve Martino & Associates, landscape architects and planners of Scottsdale, Arizona.

For an arid region that some consider wasteland, the desert boasts a surprising number of species that can provide richness and interest in home landscapes. In addition to the many cacti, agaves, and yuccas, there are shrubs like desert broom, red-wing hop bush, red bird of paradise, feathery cassia, chuparosa, and firecracker plant—the latter two bearing red or orange tubular flowers that are special favorites of hummingbirds. Ground covers suitable for lawns and meadows include blue grama grass; galleta grass; and buffalo grass, which grows only 4 to 6 inches high, requires no mowing, and uses a quarter of the water needed to sustain Kentucky bluegrass.

The region's wildflowers, moreover, are nothing short of spectacular. Some of the perennials and annuals included in a popular "desert mix" offered by Plants of the Southwest in Santa Fe, New Mexico, are sand verbena, desert marigold, aster, brittlebush, lupine, penstemons, poppies, evening primrose, and Mojave bluebells. Equally colorful (and colorfully named) varieties for high plains gardens are blue flax, chocolate flower, firewheel, yellow coneflower, skyrocket, gay feather, and Mexican hat.

In courtyards and around the entrances to homes, there are many places where both drought-resistant plants and those that need some watering will thrive in the southwestern climate. Shown here are scenes from several gardens, including raised beds framed by a doorway (right), as well as bright-hued vines and other flourishing plants.

Cooling Courtyards

ONE TYPE of garden especially appropriate to the Southwest is the courtyard or patio, whose design still reflects the influence of the Spaniards who settled here in the sixteenth century. When the conquistadors marched north from Mexico in the 1500s to establish New Spain, their worst enemy was not the Indians but the desert sun; beating down upon their metal helmets, it was said, it was hot enought to fry their brains.

As Spaniards colonized the region, they built their houses as refuges from the heat and blowing dust, using thick adobe walls to retain the coolness of the night by day, and to store the lingering warmth of the sun for comfort on chilly nights. (Even today, adobe homes are comfortable and energy-efficient, seldom requiring air conditioning and needing little in the way of central heating.)

Making life even more pleasant in New Spain, at least for those who could afford them, were central garden courtyards patterned after those in Spain, which in turn had been adapted from earlier Persian and Islamic models and developed into such famous gardens as those of the Alhambra and

Generalife. The Spanish borrowed from the Moors many of their courtyard details, including central fountains, tiled paving in geometric patterns, and surrounding arcades that acted as cool, shady passages between rooms. From such interior gardens came the term *patio*. The Spanish word originally meant an enclosed courtyard open to the sky, but now is employed to describe almost any paved and

A prototype for courtyards in the Southwest is the tiled patio of the restored Spanish Governor's Palace in San Antonio, Texas (far left). Enclosed by vine-covered walls rimmed with broad-leaved banana plants, it focuses on a central fountain and live oak tree. Modern gardens in Arizona (below) make similar use of sheltering walls, plantings and water to create refuges from the heat.

In his own Mission-style home in Tucson, landscape architect Richard William, who calls his firm "Oasis Gardens," filled the entrance court (above) with a profusion of potted plants—Cape honeysuckle, bird of paradise, Spanish bayonet, a small orange tree, and other flowers—that flourish in the shade of a paloverde tree. In another walled backyard garden, which centers on a paved terrace and a traditional Mexican stone fountain (below and right), William planted a ground cover of vinca major and small sago palms beneath mesquite and blue willow gum trees.

planted area adjacent to a home that is used for relaxing outside.

One of the oldest true patios in the Southwest is that of the Governor's Palace in San Antonio, Texas, where shady, vine-covered arcades, bright flowers, and decorative mosaic paving center on a raised pool and fountain whose jets lend soothing music and a feeling of coolness to the air. Charming garden courts of similar inspiration can be seen in the French Quarter of New Orleans, built by early French settlers, and in other cities as well.

In the Southwest, courtyard gardens are still likely to incorporate such elements as adobe or plastered walls, tile paving, and wrought-iron gates. A small fountain or pool is often placed in the center, and bougainvillea or other vines are trained over pergolas to shade a sitting area adjoining the house. Clay pots and planters, massed around the fountain or scattered elsewhere on the patio, feature lantana, geraniums, oleander, and petunias, which add welcome dashes of color to these tranquil courtyards. The sculptural forms of aloes and agaves, with their gray-green or blue-green leaves, may also be used to add drama and cool colors to the scene.

At far left, a copper fountain shaped like a yucca plant by sculptor Lee Blackwell in a Phoenix garden designed by landscape architect Greg Trutza. At Las Palmas, a private retreat above the city, a single jet arches into a waterlily pool (left, above). In another Arizona garden, a fountain takes the form of a snake.

Desert Oases

"THERE IS a recent trend to want Arizona to look like Arizona," quips Phoenix landscape architect Steve Martino, whose award-winning gardens have helped promote the idea. Working with architects and homeowners who share his beliefs, he has created landscapes that are not only practical but that evoke both the region's Spanish heritage and the startling beauty of the desert itself.

"It's a matter of learning from the land," Martino continues. "Love for

The home of Cliff and Marilyn Douglas outside Phoenix, landscaped by Steve Martino, centers on a terrace and swimming pool, framed by agaves and wildflowers at left. An open, curving staircase leads to a rooftop deck with a view of the pool and the mountains beyond (below).

the desert has not always enjoyed a high priority here, and its fragile beauty has often been violated. That's like squandering your inheritance. If architecture, and landscape architecture, are to be of any significance in this region, they must respond to, and enhance, the desert environment. A house and its gardens should look as though they belonged to their site as naturally as the surrounding trees."

Like others living in the arid Southwest, Martino thinks of a garden as an "oasis." The concept, he notes, is not unlike that of the Spanish hacienda, where the plantings corresponded to the availability of water. At the center was the courtyard or patio, with its well or fountain as the oasis or source, a sheltered place where flowering displays of moisture-loving plants could be enjoyed at close range. As one moved farther from the source of water the plants became fewer until native, drought-tolerant vegetation took over, a guide Martino uses in most of his designs. A natural model for landscaping the middle ground between the two, he feels, is the desert wash or arroyo, where an array of different plants is concentrated as a result of periodic rains.

These three homes all won awards from the Arizona Landscape Contractors Association for their planting designs. Below: the residence of Leonard Bodell, designed by Landscaping by André. At right, above: the Ronald Niven home, by the same designer. At right, below: the Richard Hallick residence, by Margaret West.

In contemporary versions of the hacienda, the focus is usually a backyard with a swimming pool, landscaped and furnished for outdoor enjoyment and, if possible, oriented toward a striking desert view. Surrounded by smooth concrete or tile, many such pools are constructed in varied geometric shapes whose irregular angularity provides a counterpoint to the lines of the houses and the surrounding desert landscape.

As a first step in landscaping any new home, Steve Martino tries to inventory all the trees and other native plants worth saving on a site, salvaging what he can and reusing it, either in place or transplanted to more advantageous spots. A dividend of this approach is that the desert and its wildlife are minimally disturbed. Hummingbirds, rabbits, squirrels, and other residents continue to occupy their accustomed habitats, enlivening the landscape in sometimes unexpected ways. In one house, the owners note with some satisfaction, even the wild pigs called javelinas occasionally venture up on the terrace—putting their snouts to the dining room windows to see what's going on inside.

A lighted swimming pool, bordered by colorful plantings and patterned squares of grass, dramatizes an evening view of the mountains in Joel and Karen Levitz's modern Tucson home. The garden was designed by landscape architect Jeffrey Van Meren of Oasis Gardens.

The West Coast

7

IN CLIMATE and topography, America's West Coast is not so much a single region as several different ones with a common border, the Pacific Ocean. Southern California is subtropical—in places dry and desert-like but, with irrigation, an area hospitable to citrus fruits and waving palms. The rolling hills of the middle coast enjoy a mild, Mediterranean climate, conditions in which a broad range of plants will grow. Oregon and Washington are cooler and wetter—notable for rain forests, streams, and waterfalls that support a profusion of woodland and mountain plants.

Culturally, too, this is a region of great diversity. In southern California, visible echoes of the early Spanish missions and ranchos abound; the San Francisco Bay Area is cosmopolitan in its gardening tastes, while the Northwest has developed traditions of its own. In all these sub-regions, the influence of the Pacific Ocean is felt, not only in its moderating effects on coastal climates, but in exotic plants first brought from places like Australia and China, and in ancient landscaping principles imported from Japan and adapted to modern needs. Perhaps the single most pervading characteristic of the West Coast, however, is an air of openness, a love of the outdoors and a receptivity to new ideas—the kind of adventurous spirit that has always beckoned people to America's promised land. In no small way, that spirit helped bring about on the West Coast the first truly significant American innovation in landscape design: the California Style.

A colorful array of drought-resistant shrubs and flowers adorns a garden in the hills above Berkeley, California.

(189)

Far left: Orange Siberian wallflower and yellow perennial allysum stand up to the salt air in Bodega Bay, California. Near left: a field of Peruvian lilies in Berkeley. Above: ferns and wildflowers in the woods of the Northwest.

The California Style

MORE THAN four decades ago, in 1948, there appeared on the cover of *House Beautiful* magazine a garden quite unlike any seen before. In fact, it did not seem so much a garden as a many-faceted sculpture—a curving, free-form swimming pool with a curving, free-form island in the middle; a contrasting checkerboard of wooden decking; and, tying the whole to its larger natural setting, magnificent old live oak trees that framed a view of curving creeks meandering through salt marshes in the distance.

Fashioned out of a hilltop in Sonoma, California, the garden was not only a rare work of landscape art. It represented a collaboration among adventurous clients, the Dewey Donnells, and a team of equally adventurous designers: landscape architects Thomas Church and his younger associate Lawrence Halprin; architect George Rockrise; and sculptor Adaline Kent, who shaped the pool's island sculpture as a whimsical plaything that swimmers could dart through under-water or use as a comfortable, contoured platform on which to stretch out in the sun.

The Donnells' hilltop soon became one of the best-known, most photographed of modern gardens, and a major influence on landscape design. Perhaps more than any other, it marked the arrival of the so-called California Style.

Views of the Dewey Donnell pool on a Sonoma, California hilltop, designed by Thomas Church and Lawrence Halprin. The free-flowing shape of the pool and its sculpture, which show strong influences from modern art, marked a sharp break from the rigid lines and ornate details of traditional landscape design.

That style, fostered by Church, Halprin, and an increasing number of other landscape architects, was partly a revolt against the rigid European formality that dominated the Country Place Era of the early 1900s (see Chapter One for some examples of that style). The Country Place style was very predictable in its handling of site problems, and executed on a grand scale for the huge estates of wealthy eastern families, for public parks, and for urban residential areas. A group of landscape architecture students at Harvard, who were later to become very influential in the field, began to question the tenets of the Country Place style about the same time that Thomas Church was designing his innovative gardens in California. The new style that emerged sprang also from a desire to make gardens more usable, comfortable, pleasant, and practical for ordinary people, who were beginning to discover the joys of the outdoors as never before.

The California Style filled their needs. Uncluttered and functional, the designs were made for small lots that homeowners could maintain themselves. Their purpose was to provide convenient, functional space for outdoor entertaining and recreation. The gardens usually included a patio, terrace, or deck; a swimming pool; play space for children; and service areas for tool storage, trash disposal, and other such necessities. Thomas Church's gardens of the 1940s were the first examples of the California School, and the style still exists in somewhat modified form today.

Two gardens by pioneering California landscape architect Thomas Church, blend modern design with an Oriental feeling suited to the West Coast. At far left: a suburban garden built around an angular swimming pool. Below: the charming entrance to Church's own house in San Francisco.

Landscapes to Live In

"GARDENING in close conjunction with houses is not so much a separate art as a sort of outdoor architecture," wrote critic Henry-Russell Hitchcock in introducing the influential 1937 Exhibition of Landscape Architecture at the San Francisco Museum of Fine Arts.

The architectural concept of gardens as outdoor living space was born partly of necessity. While cities and suburbs spread and home ownership grew through the 1940s and '50s, both the sizes of lots and the houses built on them diminished in the face of rising costs. To give small houses a greater feeling of space and light, rooms were opened up to flow into one another inside, and opened to the outdoors through picture windows and walls of glass. Pressed into service, backyards became not just gardens to look at but gardens to live in—places to give parties, barbecue steaks, play, or simply relax under the California sky.

Two city backyards in San Francisco (far left and left, above) were designed by Thomas Church to provide maximum enjoyment on long, sloping plots only 17 feet wide, with sitting decks, a gazebo, and lush plantings threaded by paths and steps. A patio by Josephine Zeitlin (left, below) permits dining by an outdoor fire. At near left: a gardener swings in a hammock among flowerbeds.

With the notion of a garden as a place to be lived in emerged another new concept of design: a garden should not be built around a single viewpoint from the house, with a "beginning" and an "end," but should be pleasing to observe from any spot within it. The results of this revolutionary approach are evident today, all over the United States.

To make outdoor rooms more usable and easier to maintain, their floors are often paved or decked over in areas of high use; in areas of lesser use, grass gives way to decorative, ground-covering plants that do not have to be constantly mowed. Walls, fences, or hedges are arranged to define boundaries like those of indoor rooms, to separate smaller areas for different uses within the larger space, and to provide privacy from close neighbors. In addition to trees, pergolas or vine-covered trellises often function as "ceilings" to provide a further sense of enclosure and to shade sitting areas from hot sun. Seating for outdoor rooms often takes the form of built-in benching or wide copings on the edges of raised planting beds.

Not least of all, the idea of a live-in garden spawned some of California's more famous contributions to the American scene: the backyard swimming pool and its smaller cousin, the hot tub or spa, as well as the extension of usable outdoor spaces onto wooden platforms and flying decks.

California gardens are noted for their outdoor liveability, which often combines decorative plantings with features that make the spaces easier to use and enjoy. Below: a rustic bench in a sea of California poppies and yellow irises; raised beds around a fountain. At right: an arbor covered with flowering vines.

Treehouses for Grownups

"CIVILIZATION has moved us out of trees and into houses, yet the magic of life in the tree tops persists," wrote Thomas Church.

On hillsides from San Diego to Se-attle, homeowners have borne him out. Capitalizing on a seeming defect—lack of level ground—they have hung their gardens in the air on flying decks, which not only dramatize the views inherent in such sites but create space for outdoor living, too. Seating is often built into protective railings around the perimeter of the deck. In the absence of ground-level garden beds, flowers or vegetables are grown in pots or tubs. Made of durable native redwood or cedar, the decking itself—its boards spaced slightly to let rainwater drain quickly away—provide pleasing patterns and a resilient surface that, unlike masonry paving, is never noticeably hot or cold underfoot.

A redwood garden deck with seating built around a gnarled live oak (below) provides a San Anselmo, California, family with space for relaxing, sunbathing, and entertaining. Outside a screened porch in Pacific Palisades (right), a smaller deck features built-in redwood benches.

Wooded slopes present even more theatrical possibilities: creating gardens literally out of treetops. The beauty of branches and leaves can be admired close up; the foliage also frames the sky and distant scenes, seeming to give them greater clarity and depth. If trees are near enough the house, the decking can be built around them, allowing their trunks to poke through. Their crowns, close overhead, create a sheltering canopy that shades sitting and dining areas from the brilliant sun.

Such modern treehouses, as appealing to adults as they are to children, are magical places indeed, for stretching out in a hammock with a book, watching the birds, or just gazing off into space.

. . . .

On a hillside in San Rafael, California, a curving deck with a handsome redwood railing. (left). A bench-rimmed deck, nestled in a eucalyptus grove in La Jolla (above).

Native Plants for Dry Climates

A GROWING problem for gardeners in the West, as in other rapidly urbanizing regions, is a shortage of water, made especially acute in years of drought. In some areas, dry seasons drastically reduce the amount of water available for "nonessential" uses like swimming pools, and even curb what can be devoted to lawns and planting beds.

As a result, a significant trend in garden design in this part of the country is toward plants that can get along without abundant moisture. This often means reducing or eliminating areas devoted to lawn, where the grass not only must be heavily watered to survive hot summers but also must be regularly fertilized, weeded, and mowed—chores that to many homeowners have become tiresome in any case. Increasingly popular substitutes for lawn grasses are low-growing ground covers like ivy or ice plant, which, once they have become established, form a dense, attractive mat of foliage that needs little care. Walks, sitting areas, and other places that get heavy use can be covered with paving, decking, gravel, wood chips, or other durable materials.

Drought-tolerant plants, grouped in raised beds of rock, put on a striking show at Strybing Arboretum in San Francisco's Golden Gate Park. This garden of succulents, or water-storing plants, includes both native and exotic species. Some are notable for their extravagant foliage, others for spikes or clusters of brilliant flowers.

Savvy gardeners have found that another way to save both water and labor is to use tough, drought-tolerant larger plants, particularly native shrubs and trees that have evolved in adaptation with local climates. These sturdy natives are especially valuable when planted away from the house, where they can get along by themselves; only in protracted periods of drought is it necessary to drag a hose out to the perimeter of the lot to keep them alive. More delicate water-dependent species and exotic flowers can be kept in garden beds or pots nearer the house, where they are easier to keep an eye on and to water when they begin to wilt. A corollary is to group plants in any given area with an eye to their common needs for water, as well as amount of sun and type of soil. This approach is apt to result in a more natural-looking arrangement, since plants with similar requirements usually occur together in the wild.

A further means of conserving water—and avoiding the tedious handwork of watering with a hose—is to install a drip irrigation system, a network of small flexible plastic pipes and nozzles connected to an outdoor faucet and buried in the ground or snaked inconspicuously under the foliage of planting beds. Such a system, which can be adjusted to drip or spray at varying rates, not only uses as little as half the water of conventional sprinkling, but benefits plants by soaking deeper into the soil around their roots. The drip system can also be fitted with an attachment that automatically injects liquid fertilizer into the water supply, and a timer that can be set to turn the water on and off.

. . . .

On a hillside in El Cerrito, north of Berkeley, overlooking San Francisco Bay, artist Harland Hand created a colorful, personal vision of a garden (above) with species suited to the climate that he collected during travels around the world. At Big Sur, a drought-resistant border features silvery santolina and purple (native) sage.

Plants that conserve scarce water have gained the attention of gardeners. Above: flowering succulents in the garden of Harland Hand. Top right: a native-plant garden designed by Ron Lutsko, with the oranges of California poppies and the lavenders of ceanothus, sage, and woolly blue curls. Bottom right: orange nasturtiums growing on stone walls above the Pacific. Far right: brilliant plantings in the Hand garden.

Inspirations from the Orient

WHILE Japanese gardens have been admired and reproduced in many parts of this country, they have had a special, permeating influence on West Coast landscape design. Part of the reason lies in cultural and trade ties that bind the region to the Far East. It was such ties that led Portland, Oregon, to establish a "sister city" relationship with the city of Sapporo, Japan, in 1959, and four years later for the Japanese Garden Society of Oregon to begin building Portland's

Japanese Garden on a 5½ acre site above downtown, looking out on a spectacular view of the city's own "Fuji," Mount Hood.

Designed by Takuma Tono, a distinguished landscape architect from Sapporo, the garden—recognized as one of the finest in the United States—comprises five distinct landscape forms traditional in Japan: a flat garden, a tea garden, a strolling pond garden, a natural garden, and an abstract garden composed only of rocks set on a "sea" of rippled sand. Each in its own manner exemplifies the subtle beauty and tranquility that are the hallmarks of Japanese garden art.

West Coast landscape architects were among the first to recognize such attributes, and to incorporate them into contemporary gardens in various

ways. Among the principles most appealing to modern designers has been the Japanese notion of distilling from nature its essential elements and arranging them in a sort of shorthand to symbolize and suggest, to encourage the observer to admire each element individually, and to complete the scene in his mind's eye.

Three basic materials are used: rocks, carefully chosen for their sculptural or symbolic qualities; water,

The Japanese Garden in Portland, Oregon, includes a pond garden (below), and a pavilion garden of gravel raked in patterns to suggest the sea, with "islands" shaped like a sake cup and gourd to symbolize happiness (right, above). Near the tea garden (right, below), a classic "deer scare" drips water from one bamboo pipe into another, which fills, tilts, and thumps on an urn in an endless cycle.

either real or implied by an arrangement of stones, gravel, and perhaps a bridge to suggest a stream bed or pool; and plants, including meticulously trained and pruned evergreens, lacy maples, and gracefully waving bamboos. Though plants like azaleas and irises are enjoyed during their blooming period, a Japanese garden does not rely on splashy displays of flowers for major interest, but rather on an underlying structure of forms that is a pleasure to observe at any season of the year.

Elements of these gardens are arranged asymmetrically, but in balance, to create a sense of privacy and serenity, a refuge from the crowded, hectic world outside. This feeling of tranquility makes the Japanese approach particularly suited to the smallest city or suburban lots. Often adding to the effect is a sense of mystery as well as calm in Oriental-style gardens. A path may disappear around a corner, its destination concealed from visitors, drawing them on to explore, and making small garden spaces seem larger than they are.

In southern California, Takeo Uesugi designed a modern version of a Japanese stroll garden around a swimming pool and spa (above), with decorative carp animating a pond beneath a waterfall (far left). A garden on a lake in Oregon (left) shows Oriental influence in its use of rocks and water set off by flowering trees.

Northwestern Gardens

THE CLIMATE of the Pacific Northwest is unlike that of any other part of the United States. Temperatures moderated by warm ocean currents combine with abundant rainfall and high levels of humidity to make the region one of the world's great natural gardening spots. Because the weather is similar to that of England, gardeners can grow many favorites of British flower gardens. Plants such as primroses and delphiniums, for example, which are difficult to grow in many parts of the United States, flourish in the moist, cool climate of the Northwest.

Northwestern forests are full of towering evergreens, ferns, and ground covers. In the rain forests along the Columbia River, the frequent rainfall supports mosses that are half a foot thick in some places. The Pacific Northwest hosts a diversity of wildflowers well suited to garden use, too, including buttercups, columbine, dame's rocket, penstemon, monkey flower, storksbill, phlox, lu-

Right: Stone steps ascend a richly landscaped hillside at Bishop's Close, the Portland, Oregon garden of Peter Kerr. Far right: a mountain waterfall gushing among mossy trunks and wildflowers in Oregon's Columbia River Gorge.

pines, foxgloves, rabbit brush, salal, and bitterroot.

Many of the plants growing in the wild on mountainsides and along the Pacific Coast are unique to the Northwest and are found nowhere else. The region has been a rich source of plants introduced to the horticulture industry. As is the case throughout most of the United States, development is encroaching on the wild places of the Northwest. But many of the residents are ecology-minded and efforts are being made to preserve these irreplaceable habitats.

A particularly well-loved trademark of the Northwest is the rhododendron, among the most magnificent of flowering evergreen shrubs. Indeed, greater numbers of more different varieties are probably grown in Oregon and Washington than anywhere else. One reason is that the region provides ideal conditions for their special needs: a moist, mild climate, naturally rich, acid soils, and forest shade that protects the plants from hot summer sun.

Rhododendrons work beautifully in woodland gardens, where they can be underplanted with wildflowers, ferns,

and mosses. The large clusters of flowers, ranging from pastel pink to brilliant magenta to snowy white, show to advantage against the plants' glossy leaves, and especially in front of a backdrop of dark woods. In the garden shown on these pages, for example, both the rhododendrons and wildflowers are played against a setting of tall native firs and birches that

Far left: rhododendrons in the Kerr garden. Below: the Oregon garden of Cecil and Molly Smith, noted for its rhododendron collection. A white yakushimanum hybrid, with yellow laburnum, is seen in close-up at left.

have been carefully pruned to admit the pearly light of often-overcast skies.

Located near Portland, Oregon, the garden was created over a period of forty years by a well-known rhododendron breeder and his wife—Cecil and Molly Smith. The garden contains some of the hybrids Mr. Smith introduced (the vibrant pink "Relaxation" and the self-descriptive "Yellow Star" among them), as well as varieties developed by other prominent hybridizers. There are also species native to the Northwest, and others from remote places as far-flung as the Himalayas and the Japanese island of Yakushima. Underplantings of club mosses, trilliums, bunchberry, western sword ferns, and other native plants help integrate the rhododendrons into their dramatic woodland setting.

Views of the Cecil and Molly Smith garden in Oregon, where more than 600 species and varieties of rhododendrons thrive. They range in color from whites and pinks to purples and reds, and are displayed in a lovely forest setting of birches and firs, along with flowering cherry trees, trilliums, anemones, primroses, ferns, laburnums and other native northwestern and exotic woodland plants.

Evergreens and Rocks

IN THE Pacific Northwest, where forests of native Douglas firs reach 200 feet toward the sky, evergreens are the kings of plants, and it is not surprising that they play a dominant role in garden design. Evergreen trees and shrubs, both native and exotic, can be seen in many of the region's gardens, serving not only as year-round focal points in themselves, but as dark, contrasting backdrops that heighten the intensity of seasonal flower dis-

plays. No less a theme is the use of rocks, the natural companions of evergreens on mountainsides.

The highly sculptural qualities of certain evergreen species are nicely dramatized in a garden located in the hills above the Willamette River in Portland, Oregon. Developed over a period of more than forty years by its owners, Jane and John Platt, its central feature is an "island" rock garden floating in a sea of green lawn, which in turn is surrounded by taller boundary plantings of evergreens.

Framed by old apple trees saved from a former orchard, the rock garden was built with two- and three-ton rocks that the Platts found in a quarry on the slopes of Mount Hood and hauled to the site with the help of a

rented crane and flatbed truck. Today the garden serves as a setting for an outstanding collection of dwarf conifers, punctuated by the handsome conical shapes of Alberta spruces, the pencil-thin accents of cedars of Lebanon, and a host of smaller species, including American arborvitaes of a richly textured golden hue. Beneath these grow many alpine and woodland plants: trilliums, hepaticas, lady's slippers, dwarf irises, and saxifrages.

Plantings of evergreens and azaleas adorn the Oregon garden of Jane and John Platt, whose house is set among the apple trees of a former orchard (above). The focal point is a sloping rock garden with a superb collection of dwarf conifers (right above and below), including conical Alberta spruces and golden arborvitaes. A sinuous weeping redwood stands on the lawn.

An even more spectacular garden based on evergreens and rocks overlooks the Columbia River Valley in Washington. This stunning landscape takes its cue entirely from nature, not from man, and it eloquently demonstrates how far American garden design has evolved in time and space from the orderly dooryards of New England. It is a rock garden, in a sense—except here the rocks are not small stones placed in someone's backyard for picturesque effect. They are the real thing: the craggy foothills of the Cascade Range.

The garden was started as a labor of love by Herman Ohme, a native of the Illinois flatlands who had become entranced by the mountain scenery of the West. An outdoorsman, he settled in the Columbia River Valley near Wenatchee, Washington, and worked in a local fruit orchard, spending as much time as he could hiking in the nearby Cascades. In 1929 Ohme married and bought 40 acres of his own, which included a dry, rocky bluff on which not much grew except a scattering of desert sage.

While getting an orchard started on the lower land, Herman and his bride Ruth often climbed up to the high ground to admire the view. One day he turned to her and said, pointing to his favorite peaks in the distance, "You know, this spot could be made as beautiful as the mountains over there."

On a barren hillside above the Wenatchee Valley, Herman and Ruth Ohme created their own idealized version of Western mountain scenery, planting thousands of little firs, cedars and hemlocks that they had dug in the nearby Cascades, and splashing the ground beneath them with drifts of alpine flowers, including pink phlox, blue bugleweed and white rock cress.

They were soon making trips to the Cascades in their little coupe, returning with the first of more than a thousand small firs, red cedars, and hemlocks loaded into the rumble seat. To insure the survival of their newly planted specimens, they dug ditches for pipelines and a sprinkler system that would bring water up from the valley below With the help of an old mule and a homemade wooden sled, Mr. Ohme rearranged rocks, built stone pathways, and grubbed out the sage, replacing it with areas of green and flowering ground covers, including drifts of pink creeping phlox, thyme, dianthus, sedums, and sagina moss. He also harnessed the mule to a drag bucket to excavate the first of several pools that, like the rest of the landscape, look so natural one would think they had always been there.

The Ohmes' efforts began to attract attention, and a decade later, at the urging of admirers, they opened their alpine oasis to the public. Under the care of their son Gordon, his wife Carol, and their sons, it has since grown to 9 acres, attracting some thirty thousand visitors a year to climb the mountain paths, look out across the bountiful valley, and rejoice in the beauty that Herman and Ruth Ohme envisioned half a century ago.

. . . .

Sixty years after it was started, the Ohme garden looks timeless. Rocks, trees and wildflowers, the garden's basic ingredients, reflect an American urge to return to the land.

Gardens Open to the Public

MANY NOTABLE gardens in the United States welcome visitors. Gardens open to the public range from major botanical gardens to small historic plots maintained by local volunteers. A sampling follows, with emphasis on historic gardens, regional garden types, and displays of native plants. Hours and admission fees vary, and not all the gardens are open year-round, so it is wise to check in advance.

More complete listings are given in regional and national guidebooks to public gardens. Local garden clubs, horticultural societies, and historical associations are other good sources of information. Many of these groups sponsor trips to public gardens, tours of private gardens, and lectures on garden history and design.

The Northeast

CONNECTICUT

Coventry. *Caprilands Herb Farm,* Silver St.
Some thirty different kinds of herb gardens; guided tours, lunches, gift shop.

Farmington. *Stanley Whitman House,* High St.
Restored Colonial home with flower and herb gardens.

Hartford. *Butler-McCook Homestead,* High St.
Formal nineteenth-century garden with parterres of perennials and roses.
   Elizabeth Park, Prospect Ave.
Oldest municipal rose garden in the United States, with hundreds of varieties and thousands of plants. Wildflower, rock, and herb gardens.

Higganum. *The Sundial Herb Garden,* Brault Hill Rd.
A re-creation of a seventeenth-century knot garden, a traditional eighteenth-century herb garden, and a topiary garden. Herb shop and tea room.

Litchfield. *White Flower Farm,* Rte. 63.
Display gardens of perennials and other plants; greenhouses, nurseries, retail shop.

New Canaan. *Olive Lee Memorial Garden,* Chichester Rd.
Woodland garden with many varieties of azaleas, rhododendrons, and native wildflowers.
   New Canaan Nature Center, Oenoke Ridge Road.
Herb and wildflower gardens, woodland trails, modern solar greenhouse.

New London. *Connecticut College Arboretum,* Williams St.
Outstanding collections of native trees, hollies, heaths, viburnums, rhododendrons, laurels, wildflowers.

Norfolk. *Hillside Gardens,* Litchfield Rd.
Perennial beds and borders displaying seasonal color; nursery, plant shop.

Stamford. *Bartlett Arboretum,* Brookdale St.
Specimen trees, dwarf conifers, rhododendrons, azaleas; bog, woodland, demonstration gardens.

Waterford. *Harkness Memorial State Park,* Rte. 213
A 1902 mansion with formal gardens, topiary, rock garden, greenhouses.

Wethersfield. *Webb-Deans-Stevens Museum,* Main St.
Three restored eighteenth-century houses and gardens.

MAINE

Camden. *Merryspring,* Conway Rd., off Rte. 1
A 66-acre horticultural center emphasizing shrubs, trees, and wildflowers native to Maine.
Merry Gardens, Mechanic St.
A mail-order nursery that displays flowering and foliage plants on its grounds.

Mount Desert Island.
The opulent private gardens of summer residents are not generally open to the public, though some may be visited on tours organized by local garden clubs. Notable gardens that welcome visitors include *Thuya Lodge* and the *Asticou Azalea Garden* in Northeast Harbor; the latter is known for its azaleas, rhododendrons, and Japanese sand garden.
Wild Gardens of Acadia, Sieur de Monts Spring.
Outstanding collection of wildflowers and other native plants displayed in beach, meadow, and bog habitats.

MASSACHUSETTS

Boston. *Arnold Arboretum,* Jamaica Plain
Renowned collection of trees and shrubs for the North Temperate Zone, including both native species and plant-hunters' finds from around the globe. Spectacular displays of cherries, crab apples, hawthorns, magnolias, native azaleas, dwarf conifers.

Framingham. *Garden in the Woods,* Hemenway Rd.
On 45 acres, the New England Wildflower Society maintains the largest landscaped collection of native plants in the Northeast, displayed in woodland, meadow, and water habitats. Courses, trips, educational materials also offered.

Ipswich. *John Whipple House,* South Main St.
Restored 1640 house with herb, rose, and flower gardens featuring species used in the seventeenth century.

Plymouth. *Plimoth Plantation,* Rte. 3A
Authentic re-creation of the first New England settlement, with dwellings and vegetable and herb gardens surrounded by a defensive stockade.

Quincy. *Adams National Historic Site,* Adams St.
Lived in by four generations of Adamses, this 1731 house has a charming mid-nineteenth-century perennial garden and a small orchard.

Salem.
Several historic gardens are worth a visit, including those of the *Essex Institute,* the *Ropes Mansion,* and the *House of the Seven Gables.*

Stockbridge. *Berkshire Garden Center,* Rtes. 102 and 183
Rock, rose, perennial, herb, and vegetable gardens; orchard; garden for the handicapped; bog and water plants.
The village of Stockbridge is prettily planted and some of it is maintained as a nineteenth-century town. Gardens of note include those of *Naumkeag* and *Chesterwood,* built as turn-of-the-century summer homes.

Sturbridge. *Old Sturbridge Village,* Rtes. I-86 and I-90
A re-created New England village of the early nineteenth century,

with vegetable, herb, and flower gardens, farming and crafts displays. An annual Garden Weekend in early August features tours and lectures.

Waltham. *Gore Place,* Rte. 20
Early nineteenth-century mansion with formal, box-edged flower gardens, and an herb garden in intricate knot patterns.

NEW HAMPSHIRE

North Hampton. *Fuller Gardens,* Willow Ave.
An estate garden of the 1920s with a large rose garden, Japanese garden, perennial borders, and wildflower walk.

Portsmouth. *Strawbery Banke,* Marcy St.
A 10-acre restoration of thirty-five historic houses including re-creations of a vegetable and herb garden of the 1720s, an elaborate Victorian garden, and a Colonial Revival garden. A New England Gardening Day, held annually in late June, features garden tours, workshops, and floral displays.
   The Moffat-Ladd House, 154 Market St.
Old-fashioned garden with formal flower beds, terraces, lilac hedges, rose arbors, an herb garden, and fruit trees.

NEW YORK

Canandaigua. *Sonnenberg Gardens,* Rte. 21
A lavish late-Victorian landscape with Italian, Japanese, rose, rock, and water gardens; specimen trees, statuary, and fountains.

Cold Spring. *Stonecrop,* Rte. 301
Splendid rock, water, and perennial gardens on a private estate; greenhouses, plant sales. Visits by appointment.

Garrison. *Boscobel,* Rte. 9D
Restored early-nineteenth-century estate with English, rose, herb gardens and an orangery.
   Other notable Hudson River estates include *Lyndhurst* in Tarrytown, the *Roosevelt* and *Vanderbilt* homes in Hyde Park, *Olana* in Hudson, and *Van Cortland Mansion* in the Bronx.

Ithaca. *Cornell Plantations,* Cornell University
Botanical garden and arboretum with wildflower trails; azaleas and rhododendrons; herb, perennial, and test gardens.

Millbrook. *Cary Arboretum,* Rte. 44
Fine collection of North American and Asian trees; Fern Glen with 125 varieties.
   Innisfree Garden, Tyrrel Rd.
An estate with natural gardens terraced on forested hills around a lake.

New Paltz. *Mohonk Mountain House Gardens,* Mohonk Lake
Victorian resort with period gardens and native wildflower trails.

New York City. *New York Botanical Garden,* Bronx Park
A 250-acre horticultural showcase especially notable for its rock garden, native plant garden, and pristine hemlock forest, as well as a magnificent Victorian conservatory housing tropical and desert plants.
   Brooklyn Botanic Garden, Washington Ave., Brooklyn
Famed for its Japanese gardens, rose garden, and flowering trees. A fine bonsai collection is housed in one of several new conservatories.
   Queens Botanical Garden, Main St., Flushing
Rose, herb, and demonstration gardens.

Wave Hill, 252nd St., Bronx
An old Hudson River estate with flower, herb, wild, water, and shade gardens; garden education center.

Old Westbury. *Old Westbury Gardens,* Old Westbury Rd.
One of the great American estate gardens of the early twentieth century, with an allée of magnificent European beeches; a walled garden; boxwood, rose, and herb gardens; Japanese garden.

Oyster Bay. *Planting Fields Arboretum,* Mill River Rd.
Another splendid relic of the "Country Place" era, with stately trees; impressive collection of rhododendrons and azaleas; conservatory with orchids, camellias, and tropical plants.

RHODE ISLAND

Bristol. *Blithewold Gardens and Arboretum,* Ferry Rd.
An 1896 mansion with rose, rock, and water gardens; large wildflower meadow.

Newport.
The gardens of several Newport mansions are worth a visit, including the formal gardens at *Rosecliff, The Breakers,* and *The Elms.*

Portsmouth. *Green Animals,* Cory's La.
Probably the finest remaining collection of topiary in the United States. More than a hundred pieces carved out of privet include geometric forms and a "zoo" with an elephant, a camel, a rabbit, and a giraffe.

Providence. *Roger Williams Park*
A 450-acre city park with lakes, formal, Japanese, and rose gardens; greenhouses, seasonal flower shows.
    Also worth seeing in Providence are the landscaping at *Swan Point Cemetery,* period gardens at the *Aldrich House, Hopkins House,* and *Shakespeare's Head.*

Westerly. *Wilcox Park,* High St.
Arboretum of dwarf conifers, herb garden with knot gardens and culinary herbs, perennial garden, and waterlily pond.

VERMONT

North Bennington. *Park-McCullough House,* West St.
Restored Victorian estate with parklike lawns; herb, perennial, and vegetable gardens; waterlily pool.

Shelburne. *Shelburne Museum,* Rte. 7
A museum of Americana housed in numerous buildings on spacious grounds with hundreds of lilacs and herb gardens of medicinal, culinary, and dye plants.

The Middle Atlantic States

DELAWARE

Greenville. *Mt. Cuba Center,* Barley Mill Rd.
Native trees, flowering shrubs, and wildflowers in woodland, field, and pond settings.

Wilmington. *Nemours,* Rockland Rd.
Created by Alfred I. du Pont, the gardens of Nemours were patterned after Versailles. Adorned by statuary and urns, they sweep grandly from a Louis XIV mansion to a fountain pool of heroic proportions, an intricate parterre garden, a huge colonnade, a sunken garden, and finally out to a "temple of love," where some fifty thousand tulips bloom each spring.
    Eleutherian Mills, Hagley Museum, Rtes. 100 and 141
The much smaller, early nineteenth-century home and French garden of the dynasty's founder, Eleuthère I. du Pont.
    Rockwood Museum, Shipley Rd.
A mid-century, Gothic-style mansion and Victorian garden.
    Wilmington Garden Day, featuring tours of more than a score of houses and gardens, is held annually on a Saturday in early May

(contact St. Andrew's Episcopal Church, 8th and Shipley Sts., Wilmington, DE 19801).

Symposia and tours of outstanding gardens are also coordinated by the *Brandywine Valley Conference* (c/o Hagley Museum, P.O. Box 3630, Wilmington, DE 19807).

Winterthur. *Winterthur Museum and Gardens,* Rte. 52
The former estate of Henry Francis du Pont, who began landscaping it in the 1920s. Perhaps America's grandest adaptation of the English naturalistic style—a skillful blending of native woodlands, fields, and wildflowers with introduced rhododendrons, azaleas, tulips, and daffodils.

DISTRICT OF COLUMBIA

Dumbarton Oaks, R and 32nd Sts., N.W.
Designed in the 1920s by Beatrix Farrand, the 16-acre former estate is regarded as America's most sensitive adaptation of Italian garden art. Includes ornate pebble garden; green and rose gardens; beech, urn, fountain, and arbor terraces; box walk, ellipse, and a miniature theater with an oval pool.

U.S. National Arboretum, New York Ave., N.E.
A 444-acre living museum of native and introduced plants, including more than two thousand cultivars of azaleas and rhododendrons, plus camellias, magnolias, evergreens, and ferns. A "New American Garden" demonstrates use of grasses, perennials, and wildflowers as alternatives to traditional foundation plantings and lawns. Also notable: Japanese Garden and bonsai collection; 2-acre National Herb Garden with large ornamental knot garden, historic roses, ten specialty gardens showing the uses of herbs.

MARYLAND

Accokeek. *National Colonial Farm,* Piscataway Park
Re-creation of mid-eighteenth-century plantation, with crop demonstrations, a kitchen garden, herb garden, orchard, barnyard, woodland trail.

Annapolis. *William Paca House and Garden,* Prince George St.
Restored home of Maryland's pre–Revolutionary War governor includes clipped English parterres; herb, rose, and wildflower gardens.

Baltimore. *Cylburn Arboretum,* Greenspring Ave.
Trails with woodland wildflowers; herb and perennial gardens; flowering shrubs and trees.

Lilypons. *Lilypons Water Gardens,* Lilypons Rd.
Waterlilies, lotuses, irises, and other plants are displayed by this leading supplier of aquatic plants and ornamental fish. An annual Lotus Blossom Festival is held in early July, a Koi Festival in early September.

Monkton. *Ladew Topiary Gardens,* Rte. 146
One of the few remaining gardens of its kind, with foliage trimmed into geometrical, human, and animal shapes.

NEW JERSEY

Far Hills. *Leonard J. Buck Gardens,* Rtes. I-287 and 512
Naturally rocky terrain transformed into outstanding alpine gardens with wildflowers, rhododendrons, and ferns.

Morristown. *Frelinghuysen Arboretum,* E. Hanover Ave.
Former estate with specimen and flowering trees, wildflower trails, azaleas and rhododendrons, peonies, ferns, bulb displays.

Also notable in Morristown are the eighteenth-century gardens of the *Wicks* and *Schuyler-Hamilton* houses and the Victorian gardens of *Acorn Hall.*

Ringwood. *Skylands,* Skylands Rd.
Mansion with formal gardens, tulips and daffodils displays, flowering crabapples; wildflower, heath, and bog gardens; woodland trails.

Somerville. *Duke Gardens,* Rte. 206
Displayed in greenhouses, the eleven garden types here cover a

wide range of eras, cultures, and climates: Indo-Persian, Chinese, Japanese, tropical, subtropical, desert, Italian, French, English, Colonial, and Edwardian.

PENNSYLVANIA

Chadds Ford. *Brandywine River Museum,* Rte. 1
Gardens of wildflowers and other native plants surround a restored nineteenth-century grist mill housing works of the Wyeth family and other regional artists.

Kennett Square. *Longwood Gardens,* Rtes. 1 and 52
One of the world's great botanical and pleasure gardens, and a major educational center, this former estate of Pierre du Pont is a landmark in early-twentieth-century opulence. Especially renowned for its fountain displays, lake, waterfalls, and lily pools, it also boasts an open-air theater. Flower walk; Italian water garden; topiary, rose, rock, and demonstration gardens; and conservatories that bloom in winter under 4 acres of glass.

Morrisville. *Pennsbury Manor,* Pennsbury Memorial Rd.
The restored estate of William Penn recalls life of the late 1600s in kitchen and herb gardens, an orchard, vineyard, and manicured formal gardens containing both English flowers and wildflowers from the surrounding woods.

Philadelphia. *Morris Arboretum,* Meadowbrook Ave., Chestnut Hill
Former Victorian estate with formal rose garden, English park, azalea meadow, holly slope, swan pond, Japanese garden, and conservatory.
  Wyck, Germantown Ave., Germantown
Historic house with gardens including a charming old rose garden.
  Bartram's Garden, 54th St. at Lindbergh Blvd.
Eighteenth-century home of famed botanist and collector John Bartram. Historic native plants include franklinia, now extinct in the wild.
  Physic Garden, 8th and Pine Sts.
Devoted to plants grown in the eighteenth century for medicinal purposes.
  Ebenezer Maxwell Mansion, West Tulpehocken St.
Victorian-era gardens.
  The Pennsylvania Horticultural Society, 325 Walnut St.
Formal eighteenth-century flower, vegetable, and herb gardens. Also sponsors tours of public and private gardens in the region.

Washington Crossing. *Bowman's Hill Wildflower Preserve,* Washington Crossing Historic State Park
Outstanding collections of wildflowers, shrubs, and trees native to Pennsylvania; lily pond, bog, walking trails.

VIRGINIA

Charlottesville. *Monticello,* Rte. 53
Thomas Jefferson's famous home, with formal flower gardens, a 1,000-foot-long vegetable garden, vineyard, orchard, wild woodland grove. A new Thomas Jefferson Center for Historic Plants features interpretive gardens, exhibits, and a shop where visitors can purchase the offspring of original Monticello plantings.
  While in Charlottesville, see Jefferson's two other masterpieces, the *University of Virginia* campus and *Ash Lawn.*

Lorton. *Gunston Hall,* Rte. 242
A historic mansion best known for its towering boxwood allée, which is more than two centuries old.

Mount Vernon. Mount Vernon Memorial Highway
Home of another talented gardener, George Washington, with flower gardens, boxwood hedges, bowling green, rose garden, kitchen garden, orchard.

Once part of Mount Vernon were nearby *Woodlawn,* an eighteenth-century mansion with a parterre garden of old roses and woodland walking trails; and *River Farm,* headquarters of the American Horticultural Society, which maintains many display gardens on its grounds and sponsors regional garden tours.

Norfolk. *Norfolk Botanical Gardens,* Airport Rd.
One of the country's largest azalea collections. Also rhododendrons, camellias, roses, hollies, heaths, and heathers. Seasonal festivals and flower shows.

Richmond.
The city boasts many historic homes and gardens, including *Maymount, Virginia House,* the *Bryan Park Azalea Garden,* and *Agecroft Hall.*

An annual *Virginia Garden Week,* in late April, is sponsored by the Garden Club of Virginia, 12 E. Franklin St., Richmond, VA 23219.

Williamsburg. *Colonial Williamsburg,* Rte. I-64
The renowned restoration of Virginia's eighteenth-century capital, with close to a hundred gardens, large and small, reflecting the Dutch-English style popular in the Colonies and planted only with species known to have been in use at the time. The gardens range from the elaborate geometrical landscapes of the Governor's Palace to smaller plots of flowers and vegetables at private homes.

Also worthy of note are nearby *Carter's Grove Plantation,* which has flower, herb, and vegetable gardens of the mid-1700s, and *Bassett Hall,* another large eighteenth-century estate.

An *Annual Williamsburg Garden Symposium,* held in early April, features talks, films, and garden tours conducted by staff horticulturists and distinguished visiting horticulturists from around the United States and abroad (contact Garden Symposium, P.O. Drawer C, Williamsburg, VA 23187).

The Southeast

ALABAMA

Birmingham. *Birmingham Botanical Garden,* Lane Park Rd.
Gardens devoted to roses, wildflowers, irises, day lilies, magnolias, ferns; Japanese garden and bonsai collection; All-America Selections garden of annuals and vegetables; home demonstration garden offering ideas for southern gardeners.

Theodore. *Bellingrath Gardens,* Bellingrath Rd.
Formal estate gardens in various styles, with spectacular displays of azaleas, camellias, roses, tulips, chrysanthemums, and many other native and exotic plants.
Arlington Historic Home and Garden, Cotton Ave.
Dating from the 1840s, has period boxwood, rose, and perennial gardens, flowering dogwoods and magnolias.

FLORIDA

Miami. *Fairchild Tropical Garden,* Old Cutler Rd.
The largest tropical botanical garden in the continental United States, with some five hundred kinds of palms, plus thousands of varieties of bromeliads, orchids, cycads, and ferns.
Villa Vizcaya, South Miami Ave.
A lavish and authentic copy of an Italian renaissance garden.

Palm Beach. *Four Arts Garden,* Royal Palm Way.
Demonstrations of how tropical and semitropical plants can be used in Florida gardens.

Sarasota. *Marie Selby Botanical Gardens,* South Palm Ave.
Outstanding collection of plants of the tropical rain forest, including orchids, bromeliads, gesneriads, and ferns.

GEORGIA

Athens. *University of Georgia Botanical Garden,* South Milledge Ave.
Many different display gardens, including trees, wildflowers, and other native Georgia plants.

Atlanta. *Atlanta Botanical Garden,* Piedmont Park
Collection of native plants; home demonstration gardens; rose, herb, and vegetable gardens.

Also in Atlanta are the *Cator Woolford Memorial Gardens,* with native trees and wildflowers, azaleas, and other displays; and restored period gardens on the *Atlanta Historical Society* grounds.

Pine Mountain. *Callaway Gardens,* Rte. 27
Many horticultural sights on 2,500 acres: trails featuring seven hundred varieties of azaleas, among them fifteen notable native ones, as well as rhododendrons, dogwoods, and wildflowers; 450 varieties of hollies, along with daffodils and camellias; thickets of native mountain laurel. The *John A. Sibley Horticultural Center,* an award-winning modern garden and greenhouse complex, offers year-round floral displays. There are more than 7 acres of demonstration vegetable gardens.

Savannah.
Famed for its landscaped public squares, Savannah also has many fine gardens open to the public, including that of the historic *Ow-*

ens-*Thomas House.* More than a score of private gardens can be seen on tours held in early April (contact Historic Savannah Foundation, 41 West Broad St., Savannah, GA 31402).

KENTUCKY

Clermont. *The Bernheim Forest, Arboretum,* and *Nature Center,* Rte. 245
Woodland and wildlife refuge with miles of trails and some 1,700 species of labeled plants, including native wildflowers, shrubs, and trees.

"Open House in Kentucky," an annual tour of homes and gardens, is held in late May.

LOUISIANA

Avery Island. *Jungle Gardens,* Avery Island Rd.
Azaleas, camellias, waterlilies, wildflowers, bamboos, and more.

Jefferson Island. *Live Oaks Gardens,* Rtes. 14 and 675
Alhambra fountain garden, camellia gardens, woodland and tropical gardens.

Many. *Hodges Gardens,* Rte. 171
A large preserve with wildlife trails and acres of gardens displaying native and exotic species popular in the South.

New Orleans. *Long Vue,* Bamboo Rd.
A former estate noted for its Spanish water garden—modeled after that of Granada's Generalife—as well as other formal gardens and collections of native plants.

MISSISSIPPI

Jackson. *Mynelle Gardens,* Clinton Blvd.
Displays of azaleas, camellias, magnolias, roses, day lilies, waterlilies, and other favorite southern plants.

Many communities around the state—among them Holly Springs, Oxford, Columbus, Vicksburg, Natchez, and Port Gibson—organize spring "pilgrimages" to fine gardens and historic homes.

NORTH CAROLINA

Chapel Hill. *North Carolina Botanical Garden,* Old Mason Farm Rd.
Devoted entirely to the native flora of the Southeast, including plants of the mountains, the piedmont sandhills, and the coastal plain. The last-named includes an outstanding display of sundews, Venus flytraps, and other insect-eating plants.

New Bern. *Tryon Palace Restoration,* Pollack St.
Former home of royal Colonial governors, landscaped as an eighteenth-century English garden. Regal entrance courtyard, ornate parterres, formal allées, kitchen garden, and a great lawn leading down to a river view. A dozen historic homes in New Bern, some with notable period gardens, are included in early-April tours.

Winnabow. *Orton Plantation,* Rte. 133
Greek Revival mansion on former rice plantation, noted for its unusual "scroll garden" with hedges in the shapes of arabesques.

Winston-Salem. *Old Salem,* Rtes. 52 and 40
Authentically restored Colonial town, founded in 1766 by Protestant Moravians. Like other English-influenced gardens of the period, Old Salem's are laid out behind the houses in rectangular beds, with walkways between, and planted with vegetables, herbs, and flowers.

SOUTH CAROLINA

Charleston. *Middleton Place,* Rte. 61
One of the earliest, and still one of the finest, formal landscaped gardens in America. Famed for undulating grass terraces, "butterfly" lakes, azalea hillside, camellia gardens, and the thousand-year-old Middleton Oak. Also the scene of outdoor concerts, festivals, and other seasonal events.

Magnolia Plantation and Gardens, Rte. 61
The quintessential southern garden of romance, maintained by the same family for three centuries. Brilliant displays of azaleas, camellias, magnolias, and other flowering shrubs and trees, all reflected in lagoons surrounded by bald cypresses and live oaks draped in Spanish moss.

Cypress Gardens, Rte. 52
Many people associate Cypress Gardens with water-ski shows and costumed southern belles, but the original 16 acres of gardens, viewed from footpaths or small, flat-bottomed boats, offer stunning displays of azaleas and other flowering subtropical plants, more than eight thousand varieties in all.

Historic Charleston.
Many of the beautiful private gardens in the old part of the city can be glimpsed during a stroll through its streets. The *Charleston Festival of Houses,* held annually from late March to mid-April, includes guided walking tours of outstanding homes and gardens. (For programs and dates, contact Historic Charleston Foundation, 51 Meeting Street, Charleston, SC 29401.) Garden tours are also given on Saturdays in early April by the Garden Club of Charleston (P.O. Box 2771, Charleston, SC 29403).

TENNESSEE

Memphis. *Memphis Botanic Garden,* Cherry Rd.
Magnolia, rose, iris, dahlia, and Japanese gardens; flowering trees, wildflowers, conservatory with orchids and bromeliads.

Nashville. *Cheekwood Botanic Garden and Fine Arts Center,* Forrest Park Drive
A botanical garden and arts center with formal and Japanese gardens; collections of day lilies, irises, wildflowers, and flowering trees.

Other notable gardens in Nashville are those of *The Hermitage,* built in 1819 as Andrew Jackson's home, and the tropical conservatory plantings of the *Opryland Hotel.*

The Midwest

COLORADO

Denver. *York Street Gardens,* York St.
The Denver Botanic Garden maintains test gardens; a low-maintenance garden; rock, rose, Japanese, and herb gardens; conservatory with orchids, bromeliads, and other tropical plants.

ILLINOIS

Chicago.
Notable is the city's extensive park system, including horticultural displays at *Garfield Park, Lincoln Park,* and *Marquette Park,* and Jens Jensen's beautifully landscaped *Columbus Park.*

Glencoe. *Chicago Botanic Garden,* Lake Cook Rd.
Among many displays are a naturalistic garden of native Illinois plants; a prairie area of wildflowers and grasses; an oak-hickory forest trail; a boardwalk tour of wetland plants; rose, perennial, and bulb gardens; children's vegetable garden; learning garden for the disabled.

Lisle. *Morton Arboretum,* East-West Tollway
A major arboretum, with a prairie restoration area, flowering crabapples and lilacs, demonstration gardens, walking trails.

Rockford. *Anderson Gardens,* Stoneridge Dr.
An authentic Japanese "pond-strolling" garden, and a re-created prairie landscape with native wildflowers and grasses.

Springfield. *Abraham Lincoln Memorial Garden,* East Lake Dr.
Designed by Jens Jensen, the gardens occupy 77 acres along the shore of Lake Springfield and are devoted entirely to trees, shrubs, and flowers native to Illinois.

INDIANA

Muncie. *Christie Woods of Ball State University,* Riverside and University Aves.
Ash-oak-hickory woods, wildflowers, bog garden, formal gardens; greenhouses with a first-rate orchid collection.

New Harmony. *Robert Lee Blaffer Trust*
A preserved nineteenth-century "utopian" community with period gardens, including rose gardens, herb gardens, and a maze.

IOWA

Butler Center. *Clay Prairie Preserve*
Small but authentic remnant of Iowa's virgin tall-grass prairie, containing bluestem and Indian grasses, shrubs like prairie rose and prairie willow, and wildflowers like purple avens, rattlesnake master, and shooting star. Maintained by the Biological Preserves Committee of the University of Northern Iowa at Cedar Falls.

Clinton. *Bickelhaupt Arboretum,* South 14th St.
Dedicated to education in the use of native plants and others suitable to the region, this family arboretum maintains plantings of many kinds of trees, shrubs, and flowers. Of special interest is a demonstration prairie of native wildflowers and grasses planted from seeds gathered by volunteers.

Des Moines. *Arie den Boer Arboretum,* Water Works Park
Outstanding displays of flowering crabapples, perennials, ornamental shrubs; waterlily and lotus pools.

Also worth visiting are the *Des Moines Botanical Center* on East River Dr. and *Ewing Park* on McKinley Rd.

KANSAS

Belle Plaine. *Bartlett Arboretum,* Rte. 55
Formal flower gardens and plantings of ornamental trees.

Wakefield. *Kansas Landscape Arboretum,* Milford Lake
Large collection of native trees; wildflower garden, meadow trail, day lilies, irises.

MICHIGAN

Ann Arbor. *Matthaei Botanical Gardens.* Dixboro Rd.
Natural landscapes of woodland, prairie, and marsh, with many wildflowers along the trails. Rose garden, knot garden of herbs, rock and perennial gardens; greenhouses with tropical plants.

Bloomfield Hills. *Cranbrook,* Lone Pines Rd.
This well-known educational and art community, built around the elegant manor house and gardens of its benefactor, George Booth, has landscaped campuses featuring the architecture of Eliel Saarinen, and the sculpture of Carl Milles set in fountain pools.

Dearborn. *Henry Ford Estate Fair Lane,* 4901 Evergreen Rd.
Henry and Clara Ford's former estate was landscaped in 1914 by Jens Jensen, the celebrated pioneer of native regional landscaping. It is now a National Historic Landmark maintained by the University of Michigan.

Detroit. *Anna Scripps Whitcomb Conservatory,* Belle Isle
Located on an island transformed into a city park, the conservatory is noted for its seasonal flower shows, and for formal gardens that include perennials and waterlily ponds.

East Lansing. *Michigan State University Campus*
Many fine plantings grace this 5,000-acre campus, which has special gardens devoted to roses, perennials, bulbs, and aquatic plants.

Grosse Pointe Shores. *Edsel and Eleanor Ford House,* 1100 Lake Shore Rd.
This splendid Jens Jensen landscape, executed in the 1920s, is notable for an open grove of majestic elms and sugar maples; a great, prairielike meadow angled for views of the setting sun; and an island landscaped as a wildlife refuge.

Mackinac Island. *Grand Hotel*
This celebrated resort, first opened to guests in 1887, has extravagant Victorian gardens that display thousands of colorful bedding plants, including begonias, marigolds, geraniums, tulips, and daffodils. Also notable are the lilac and day lily collections, English gardens, and gazebo garden.

Niles. *Fernwood Botanic Garden and Nature Center,* Range Line Rd.
An educational center for gardening and nature study, Fernwood has woodland trails, a tall-grass prairie, wildflower plantings, a vegetable garden, and other demonstration areas.

MINNESOTA

Chaska. *Minnesota Landscape Arboretum,* Rte. 5
Trails lead through rolling woodlands, fields, lakes, and marshlands on this 500-acre preserve.

Minneapolis. *Eloise Butler Wildflower Garden and Bird Sanctuary,* Bryant Ave. South
Prairie, woodland, and bog areas feature many species of indigenous plants, including colorful wildflowers.

MISSOURI

St. Louis. *Missouri Botanical Garden,* Shaw Blvd.
Best known for its dramatic "Climatron"—a geodesic dome

housing exotic plants of the tropical rain forest—and other green-houses for camellias, desert species, and Mediterranean plants. Also an authentic Japanese strolling garden; bulb, iris, and day lily gardens; English woodland, rhododendron, azalea, and rose gardens.

NEBRASKA

Lincoln. *Alice Abel Arboretum,* Nebraska Wesleyan University
A 40-acre arboretum featuring native prairie grasses, wildflowers, and shrubs. It is part of a statewide system of parks that emphasize plantings suitable to the plains.

Nebraska City. *Arbor Lodge State Park*
This 65-acre former estate of Sterling Morton, founder of Arbor Day, features the original formal gardens, plus newer gardens of prairie wildflowers and grasses.

NORTH DAKOTA

Dunseith. *International Peace Garden*
Part of a large preserve established on both sides of the United States–Canada border, with formal gardens of roses, perennials, and annuals; an arboretum; and a "floral clock."

OHIO

Akron. *Stan Hywet Hall,* North Portage Path
The former estate of Frank Seiberling, founder of Goodyear Rubber Co., features a large 1915 Tudor Revival mansion and thirty-two gardens, among them an English walled garden, rose and Japanese gardens, birch and rhododendron allées.

Cleveland. *Garden Center of Greater Cleveland,* University Circle
An unusual resource for gardeners, and the model for similar centers around the country. Features rose, herb, perennial, and Japanese gardens; exhibits, courses, garden tours, and a library.

Coshocton. *Roscoe Village,* Hill St.
Restoration of a nineteenth-century village along the Ohio and Erie Canal. Contains several gardens, notably the vegetable, herb, and flower garden of Dr. Maro Johnson, the town's first doctor, planted with species typical of the 1840s.

Mansfield. *Kingwood Center,* Park Ave. West
French Provincial mansion surrounded by seventeen different gardens, including herb, rose, iris, and day lily gardens, and 20 acres of woodlands and wildflowers.

Mentor. *Holden Arboretum,* Sperry Rd.
One of the largest and best arboretums in the country, with more than 2,000 acres of woodlands and fields. Wildflower gardens, flowering fruit trees, nut trees, lilacs, hollies, rhododendrons, and azaleas. Trails are popular with cross-country skiers in winter. Educational programs are held year-round.

WISCONSIN

Hales Corners. *Boerner Botanical Gardens,* Whitnall Park
Highlights include a collection of 400 crabapple varieties, intricate herb garden, perennial garden, trial garden for annuals and perennials, wildflower garden, and large rose garden that displays All-America selections.

Madison. *University of Wisconsin Arboretum,* Seminole Highway
A 1,200-acre arboretum that emphasizes plants and animals native to Wisconsin. Featured are a 100-acre restored prairie with 300 species, deciduous woodlands with brilliant fall colors, 250 acres of wetlands, fine collections of lilacs, crabapples, and viburnums.

Milwaukee. *Mitchell Park Conservatory,* Mitchell Park
Best known for its three large geodesic domes—one is devoted to seasonal floral displays, another houses a tropical rain forest, the third contains desert plants from around the world.

In Milwaukee's suburbs, guided tours of private gardens featuring prairie and woodland wildflowers are conducted during the last week in July and the first week in August (contact Lorrie Otto, 9701 N. Lake Dr., Milwaukee, WI 53217).

The Southwest

ARIZONA

Phoenix. *Desert Botanical Garden,* Papago Park.
A 150-acre garden widely known for its collection of native plants of the Southwest and other arid regions of the world—more than ten thousand varieties of cacti and other succulents, trees, shrubs, and wildflowers. A demonstration garden, with seasonal displays, shows how desert-adapted plants can save water and create home landscapes.

Superior. *Boyce Thompson Southwestern Arboretum,* Rte. 60
A 1,000-acre desert and woodland preserve with many species of native trees, shrubs, and wildflowers.

Tucson. *Arizona-Sonora Desert Museum,* Tucson Mt. Park
Displays and demonstration gardens of cacti and other plants (and animals) native to the Sonoran desert.

NEW MEXICO

Carlsbad. *Living Desert State Park,* Rte. 285
Thousands of varieties of cacti and other arid-region plants, many native to the Chihuahuan desert.

OKLAHOMA

Oklahoma City. *Will Rogers Park and Horticultural Garden,* N.W. 36th St.
Large rose and perennial gardens, azalea trail, native tree displays, conservatory with cacti and tropical plants.

TEXAS

Dallas. *Dallas Garden Center,* Rtes. 67 and 80
Displays of azaleas, perennials, annuals, roses, bulbs; greenhouses with orchids, bromeliads, ferns, and other tropical plants.

Fort Worth. *Fort Worth Botanic Garden,* Botanic Garden Drive
Rose, perennial, water, and Japanese gardens; displays of five hundred kinds of flowering trees.

Houston. *Bayou Bend Gardens,* Westcott St.
Former home of Ima Hogg, with English, Italian, rock, and topiary gardens; displays of camellias, magnolias, and azaleas.

San Antonio. *San Antonio Botanical Center,* Funston Place
Many garden types, including an area of native plants.
    The city is also famed for its landscaped *River Walk* downtown. *Mission Conception* has a garden planted in Spanish mission style.

The West Coast

CALIFORNIA

Arcadia. *Los Angeles State and County Arboretum,* North Baldwin Ave.
A living encyclopedia of native and exotic plants, grouped by geographical regions (Asia, Australia, Africa, Mediterranean, etc.). Demonstration gardens, orchid and begonia collections.

Berkeley. *Berkeley Botanical Garden,* Centennial Dr.
One of the top-rated university gardens, with collections from around the world.
   The Regional Parks Botanical Garden, in Tilden Regional Park, features California plants, arranged by habitats, from mountain meadows to coastal dunes.

Claremont. *Rancho Santa Ana Botanic Garden,* North College Ave.
Native California and desert species, including cacti, yuccas, wildflowers.

La Cañada. *Descanso Gardens*
The world's largest camellia collection, with tens of thousands of plants of six hundred varieties, plus historic roses, Japanese and Chinese gardens, displays of lilies, irises, fuchsias, and begonias.

Lompoc. *La Purisima Mission,* Purisima Rd.
One of California's celebrated chain of missions, with an early nineteenth-century garden.

Long Beach. *Rancho Los Alamitos,* Bixby Rd.
An early southern California garden, with Spanish-Moorish influences and later Victorian overtones. A similar garden is that of *Rancho Los Cerritos,* on Virginia Rd.

San Diego. *Balboa Park,* Laurel St.
Site of an international exposition in 1915, Balboa's Spanish-Moorish buildings have gardens to match, plus rose, English, and desert gardens; and a garden of aquatic plants. The famed *San Diego Zoo,* also in Balboa Park, is notable not only for its animals but for its plantings of exotic shrubs and trees.

San Francisco. *Strybing Arboretum,* Golden Gate Park
A first-rate arboretum, with collections of rhododendrons, magnolias, evergreens, succulents, and sections devoted to the plants of the Mediterranean, Asia, Africa, South America, Australia, and New Zealand. Demonstration gardens show homeowners how to use trees, shrubs, ground covers, and flowers. Also notable is a garden of native plants displaying everything from California and Matilija poppies to fremontias and Torrey pines.
   Near the arboretum is the *Japanese Tea Garden,* one of the earliest in this country, and the *Conservatory of Flowers,* a splendid Victorian glass house with a collection of tropical plants. Not to be missed is the rest of *Golden Gate Park,* one of the best-landscaped, and most popular, municipal parks anywhere.

San Marino. *Huntington Botanical Gardens,* Oxford Rd.
An internationally acclaimed garden, with comprehensive collections of cacti and succulents, camellias, palms, and Australian plants.

San Simeon. *Hearst Castle,* Rte. 1
William Randolph Hearst's mountaintop fairyland, surrounded by lavish terraces, statues, pools, fountains, flower gardens, and magnificent specimen trees, ranging from exotic cedars of Lebanon to native redwoods and live oaks.

Santa Barbara. *Santa Barbara Botanic Garden,* Mission Canyon Rd.
Notable for its collections of native plants, including California poppies and other wildflowers, as well as shrubs and trees.

Woodside. *Filoli Center,* Canada Rd.
An outstanding formal garden of the "Country-Place" era.

OREGON

Portland. *Japanese Garden,* Washington Park
Cited by some authorities as the finest of its kind in the United States, the garden illustrates five distinct kinds of traditional Japanese garden design.

Below the Japanese Garden is the extensive *International Rose Test Garden;* in the hills above, the *Hoyt Arboretum* displays more than six hundred species of trees.
Crystal Springs Rhododendron Garden, S.E. 28th Ave.
An outstanding collection of species and hybrid rhododendrons; judged rhododendron shows in April and May.

While in Portland, don't fail to see the *Keller Fountain, Lovejoy Fountain, Pettygrove Park,* and other imaginatively designed "people parks" downtown. Fine private gardens open to public on a limited basis are the *Berry Botanic Garden, Bishop's Close,* and *Leach Botanical Park.* South of the city, the *Cecil and Molly Smith Garden,* with spectacular rhododendron displays, offers tours on selected Saturdays in March, April, and May.

WASHINGTON

Federal Way. *The Rhododendron Species Foundation,* 32nd Ave. South
Between Seattle and Tacoma, on 24 wooded acres donated by the Weyerhauser Co., 1,800 varieties, representing 503 of the 850

known rhododendron species, are on display with companion plants. In addition to maintaining the only botanical garden devoted entirely to the rhododendron, the foundation is dedicated to halting the loss of species worldwide.

Greenbank. *Meerkerk Rhododendron Gardens,* Whidbey Island
A wide selection of hybrid and species rhododendrons, including some hybridized by the late Ann Meerkerk, grow along woodland trails on this 53-acre former estate, which also serves as a test garden for new cultivars.

Seattle. *Washington Park Arboretum,* Lake Washington Blvd. East
Famed Japanese Tea Garden rivals that of Portland, with tea house, pagoda, stone lanterns, flowering plum and cherry trees. The arboretum also has fine collections of azaleas, rhododendrons, hollies, magnolias, camellias, and lilacs.

The Seattle Conservatory, in Volunteer Park, is a grand Victorian glass house displaying orchids and other tropical flowers and palms.

Wenatchee. *Ohme Gardens,* Ohme Road.
A spectacular 9-acre alpine garden.

HAWAII

Oahu. *Foster Botanical Gardens,* North Vineyard Blvd., Honolulu
An orchid garden of ten thousand plants, plus bromeliads, palms, and other tropical trees.
Harold Lyon Arboretum, Manoa Rd., Honolulu
University of Hawaii research station, with thousands of varieties of tropical plants.
Wahiawa Botanic Garden, California Ave., Wahiawa
Palms, aroids, ferns, and native tropical plants.
Waimea Arboretum and Botanical Garden, Waimea Falls Park
A sheltered valley and waterfall preserved as nature sanctuary, with collections of plants from the Hawaiian Islands and from as far away as Madagascar and Malaysia.

Kauai. Notable are the *Olu Pua Botanical Garden and Plantation* in Kalaheo, and the *Pacific Tropical Botanical Garden* and *Allerton Gardens,* in Lawai.

Sources of Further Information

THE FOLLOWING organizations offer information on various aspects of gardening and conservation. Many publish newsletters or magazines for members, sponsor educational workshops, and organize tours. Local botanical gardens and county agricultural extension agents are other good sources of information and gardening advice.

National

American Community Gardening Association
P.O. Box 93147
Milwaukee, WI 53202

American Horticultural Society
P.O. Box 0105
Mt. Vernon, VA 22121

American Rhododendron Society
14885 S.W. Sunrise Lane
Tigard, OR 97224
(and local chapters)

American Rock Garden Society
15 Fairmead Rd.
Darien, CT 06820
(and local chapters)

American Rose Society
P.O. Box 30000
Shreveport, LA 71130
(and local chapters)

Cactus and Succulent Society of America
2631 Fairgreen Ave.
Arcadia, CA 91006

Garden Club of America
598 Madison Ave.
New York, NY 10022
(and local affiliates)

Institute for Historic Horticulture
150 White Plains Rd.
Tarrytown, NY 10591

Men's Garden Club of America
P.O. Box 241
Johnston, IA 50131
(and local affiliates)

National Council of State Garden Clubs
4401 Magnolia Ave.
St. Louis, MO 63110
(and local affiliates)

National Gardening Association
180 Flynn Ave.
Burlington, VT 05401

National Wildflower Research Center
2600 FM 973 North
Austin, TX 78725

The Nature Conservancy
1815 North Lynn St.
Arlington, VA 22209
(and state chapters)

Perennial Plant Association
249 Howlett Hall
2001 Fyffe Ct.
Columbus, OH 43210

Seed Savers Exchange
203 Rural Ave.
Decorah, IA 52101

Woman's National Farm and Garden Association
15 Fox Den Rd.
West Simsbury, CT 06092

State and Regional

Alabama Wildflower Society
Rte. 2, Box 115
Northport, AL 35476

Alaska Native Plant Society
P.O. Box 141613
Anchorage, AK 99514

Arkansas Native Plant Society
Biology Dept.
Univ. of Central Arkansas
Conway, AR 72032

Arizona Native Plant Society
P.O. Box 41206 Sun Station
Tucson, AZ 85717

California Botanical Society
Dept. of Botany
University of California
Berkeley, CA 94720

California Native Plant Society
909 12th St.
Sacramento, CA 95814

Colorado Native Plant Society
P.O. Box 200
Fort Collins, CO 80522

Connecticut Botanical Society
24 Cedarwood Lane
Old Saybrook, CT 06475

Connecticut Horticultural Society
150 Main St.
Wethersfield, CT 06109

Botanical Society of Washington
Dept. of Botany, NHB 166
Smithsonian Institution
Washington, DC 20560

Florida Native Plant Society
1133 West Morse Blvd., Suite 201
Winter Park, FL 32789

Georgia Botanical Society
P.O. Box 8882
Atlanta, GA 30306

Hawaiian Botanical Society
Botany Dept., Univ. of Hawaii
3190 Maile Way
Honolulu, HI 96822

Idaho Native Plant Society
P.O. Box 9451
Boise, ID 83707

Illinois Native Plant Society
Botany Dept.
Southern Illinois Univ.
Carbondale, IL 62901

Chicago Horticultural Society
P.O. Box 400
Glencoe, IL 60022

Iowa State Horticultural Society
State House
Des Moines, IA 50319

Kansas Wildflower Society
Mulvane Art Ctr., Washburn Univ.
17th & Jewell Sts.
Topeka, KS 66621

Louisiana Native Plant Society
11128 Woodmere Dr.
Shreveport, LA 71115

Josselyn Botanical Society
P.O. Box 41
China, ME 04926

Maryland Native Plant Society
14720 Claude Lane
Cloverly, MD 20904

Massachusetts Horticultural Society
300 Massachusetts Ave.
Boston, MA 02115

New England Wildflower Society
Garden in the Woods
Hemenway Rd.
Framingham, MA 01701

Society for the Preservation of New England Antiquities
141 Cambridge St.
Boston, MA 02114

Michigan Botanical Club
Mathaei Botanical Gardens
1800 Dixboro Rd.
Ann Arbor, MI 48105

Minnesota Native Plant Society
220 BioSci Ctr., Univ. of Minn.
1445 Gortner Ave.
St. Paul, MN 55108

Mississippi Native Plant Society
202 North Andrews Ave.
Cleveland, MS 38732

Missouri Native Plant Society
P.O. Box 6612
Jefferson City, MO 65102

Montana Native Plant Society
Botany Dept.
Univ. of Montana
Missoula, MT 59812

Northern Nevada Native Plant Society
Box 8965
Reno, NV 89507

New Jersey Native Plant Society
Frelinghuysen Arboretum
Box 1295R
Morristown, NJ 07960

Native Plant Society of New Mexico
P.O. Box 5917
Santa Fe, NM 87502

Horticultural Society of New York
128 West 58th St.
New York, NY 10019

Torrey Botanical Club
New York Botanical Garden
Bronx, NY 10458

North Carolina Botanic Garden
Univ. of North Carolina
Chapel Hill, NC 27514

Southern Garden History Association
Drawer F, Salem Station
Winston-Salem, NC 27101

Ohio Native Plant Society
6 Louise Dr.
Chagrin Falls, OH 44022

Oklahoma Native Plant Society
2435 S. Peoria
Tulsa, OK 74114

Native Plant Society of Oregon
1920 Engel Ave., N.W.
Salem, OR 97304

Pennsylvania Horticultural Society
325 Walnut St.
Philadelphia, PA 19106

Pennsylvania Native Plant Society
1806 Commonwealth Bldg.
316 Fourth Ave.
Pittsburgh, PA 15222

Rhode Island Wild Plant Society
P.O. Box 534
West Kingston, RI 02892

Tennessee Native Plant Society
Biology Dept.
Univ. of Tennessee
Knoxville, TN 37996

Native Plant Society of Texas
P.O. Box 23836-TWU Station
Denton, TX 76204

Utah Native Plant Society
3631 S. Carolyn St.
Salt Lake City, UT 84106

Virginia Wildflower Preservation Society
P.O. Box 844
Annandale, VA 22033

Association for the Preservation of Virginia Antiquities
2300 East Grace St.
Richmond, VA 23223

Washington Native Plant Society
Botany Dept.
Univ. of Washington
Seattle, WA 98105

West Virginia Native Plant Society
Herbarium, Brooks Hall
West Virginia University
Morgantown, WV 26506

Botanical Club of Wisconsin
Biology Dept.
Univ. of Wisconsin
Lacrosse, WI 54601

Bibliography

Art, Henry W. *A Garden of Wildflowers: 101 Native Species and How to Grow Them*. Pownal, VT: Storey Communications, 1986.

Art, Henry W. *The Wildflower Gardener's Guide (Northeast, Middle Atlantic, Great Lakes and Eastern Canada)*. Pownal, VT: Storey Communications, 1987.

Balmori, Diana; Diane Kostial McGuire; and Eleanor M. McPeck. *Beatrix Farrand's American Landscapes: Her Gardens and Campuses*. Sagaponack, NY: Sagapress, 1985.

Balston, Michael. *The Well-Furnished Garden*. London: Mitchell Beazley Publishers, 1986.

Beacon Hill Garden Club. *Hidden Gardens of Beacon Hill*. Boston: Beacon Hill Garden Club, Inc., 1987.

Church, Thomas D., with Grace Hall and Michael Laurie. *Gardens Are For People*. New York: McGraw-Hill Book Co., 1983.

Colonial Williamsburg Foundation. *The Gardens of Williamsburg*. Williamsburg, VA: Colonial Williamsburg Foundation, 1970.

Creasy, Rosalind. *The Complete Book of Edible Landscaping*. San Francisco: Sierra Club Books, 1982.

Crockett, James Underwood; Ogden Tanner; and the Editors of Time-Life Books. *Herbs*. Alexandria, VA: Time-Life Books, 1977.

Crockett, James Underwood and the Editors of Time-Life Books. *Landscape Gardening*. Alexandria, VA: Time-Life Books, 1971.

Crockett, James Underwood; Oliver E. Allen; and the Editors of Time-Life Books. *Wildflower Gardening*. Alexandria, VA: Time-Life Books, 1977.

De Forest, Elizabeth Kellam. *The Gardens and Grounds of Mount Vernon: How George Washington Planned and Planted Them*. Mount Vernon, VA: The Mount Vernon Ladies Association of the Union, 1982.

Doell, M. Christine Klim. *Gardens of the Gilded Age*. Syracuse, NY: Syracuse University Press, 1986.

Douglas, William Lake, et al. *Garden Design: History, Principles, Elements, Practice*. New York: Quarto/Simon & Schuster, 1984.

Downing, Andrew Jackson. *Landscape Gardening*. 10th ed. Revised by Frank A. Waugh. New York: John Wiley & Sons, 1921.

DuPont, Elizabeth N. *Landscaping with Native Plants in the Middle-Atlantic Region*. Chadds Ford, PA: Brandywine Conservancy, 1978.

Eaton, Leonard K. *Landscape Artist in America: The Life and Work of Jens Jensen*. Chicago: The University of Chicago Press, 1964.

Favretti, Rudy J. *New England Colonial Gardens*. Chester, CT: The Pequot Press, 1964.

Favretti, Rudy J. and Joy P. *For Every House a Garden: A Guide for Reproducing Period Gardens*. Chester, CT: The Pequot Press, 1977.

Favretti, Rudy J. and Joy P. *Landscapes and Gardens for Historic Buildings*. Nashville, TN: American Association for State and Local History, 1978.

Favretti, Rudy J., and Gordon P. DeWolf. *Colonial Gardens*. Barre, MA: Barre Publishers, 1978.

Garrett, Howard. *Landscape Design . . . Texas Style*. Dallas: Taylor Publishing Co., 1986.

Hedrick, U.P. *A History of Horticulture in America to 1860*. New York: Oxford University Press, 1950.

Jacob, Irene and Walter. *Gardens of North America and Hawaii— A Traveler's Guide*. Portland, OR: Timber Press, 1985.

Kourik, Robert. *Designing and Maintaining Your Edible Landscape Naturally*. Santa Rosa, CA: Metamorphic Press, 1986.

Kraft, Ken and Pat. *The Best of American Gardening: Two Centuries of Fertile Ideas*. New York: Walker & Co., 1975.

Kruckeberg, Arthur R. *Gardening with Native Plants of the Pacific Northwest: An Illustrated Guide*. Seattle: University of Washington Press, 1982.

Laurie, Michael. *An Introduction to Landscape Architecture*. New York: Elsevier Science Publishing Co., 1986.

Leighton, Ann. *Early American Gardens—"For Meat and Medicine."* Boston: Houghton Mifflin Co., 1970.

Leighton, Ann. *American Gardens in the Eighteenth Century: "For Use or for Delight."* Amherst: The University of Massachusetts Press, 1986.

Leighton, Ann. *American Gardens of the Nineteenth Century—"For Comfort and Affluence."* Amherst: The University of Massachusetts Press, 1987.

Leighton, Ann. *Early American Gardens—"For Meat and Medicine."* Boston: Houghton Mifflin Co., 1970.

Lenz, Lee W. *Native Plants for California Gardens*. Pomona, CA: Day Printing Corp., 1973.

Littlefield, Susan S.H. *Seaside Gardening*. New York: Quarto/ Simon & Schuster, 1986.

Martin, Laura C. *The Wildflower Meadow Book: A Gardener's Guide*. Charlotte, NC: East Woods Press, 1986.

Miller, Everitt L., and Jay S. Cohen. *The American Garden Guidebook (Eastern U.S. and Canada)*. New York: M. Evans and Co., 1987.

Miller, Wilhelm. *The Prairie Spirit in Landscape Gardening*. Urbana: University of Illinois, 1915.

Miller, Wilhelm. *What England Can Teach Us About Gardening*. Garden City, NY: Doubleday, Page & Co., 1917.

Morris Arboretum. *Gardens & Arboreta of Philadelphia and the Delaware Valley*. Philadelphia: Morris Arboretum, 1981.

New England Wildflower Society. *Garden in the Woods Cultivation Guide*. Framingham, MA: New England Wildflower Society, Inc., 1987.

New England Wildflower Society. *Nursery Sources: Native Plants and Wildflowers*. Framingham, MA: New England Wildflower Society, Inc., 1987.

Newton, Norman T. *Design on the Land: The Development of Landscape Architecture*. Cambridge, MA: Harvard University Press, 1971.

Ottesen, Carole. *The New American Garden*. New York: Macmillan Publishing Co., 1987.

Payne, Rolce Redard and Cymie R. *New England Gardens Open to the Public*. Boston: David R. Godine, 1979.

Ray, Mary Helen, and Robert P. Nichols, eds. *A Guide to Significant and Historic Gardens of America*. Athens, GA: Garden Club of Georgia, Agee Publishers, 1983.

Scott, Frank J. *The Art of Beautifying Suburban Home Grounds*. New York: D. Appleton & Co., 1870.

Smith, J. Robert, with Beatrice S. Smith. *The Prairie Garden: 70 Native Plants You Can Grow in Town or Country*. Madison: The University of Wisconsin Press, 1980.

Stone, Doris M. *The Great Public Gardens of the Eastern United States*. New York: Pantheon Books, 1982.

Tanner, Ogden, and the Editors of Time-Life Books. *Rock and Water Gardens*. Alexandria, VA: Time-Life Books, 1979.

Thomas, Charles B. *Water Gardens for Plants and Fish*. Neptune City, NJ: TFH Publications, 1988.

Tice, Patricia M. *Gardening in America, 1830–1920*. Rochester, NY: The Strong Museum, 1984.

Tobey, George B. *A History of Landscape Architecture: The Relationship of People to Environment*. New York: American Elsevier Publishing Co., 1973.

Verey, Rosemary, and Ellen Samuels. *The American Woman's Garden*. A New York Graphic Society Book. Boston: Little, Brown & Co., 1984.

Wilkinson, Elizabeth, and Marjorie Henderson. *The House of Boughs: A Sourcebook of Garden Designs, Structures, and Suppliers*. New York: Yolla Bolly Press/Viking Penguin, Inc., 1985.

Index

Acknowledgments

THE AUTHOR is indebted to Sarah Kirshner, Roseann Martinez, Diana Mignatti, and others at Running Heads, to Kathleen Westray and Ed Sturmer for their handsome design, and to Tom Cooper, John Barstow, Roger Swain, and Tina Schwinder of *Horticulture* magazine.

The following have also been generous with their time and ideas: Linda Askey and Bill MacDougald, *Southern Living* magazine, Birmingham, Alabama; Liz Ball, Springfield, Pennsylvania; Judy Becker, Victory Garden, WGBH-TV, Boston; Kurt Bluemel, Baldwin, Maryland; Peggy Bowditch, Philadelphia; Kathy Brenzel, *Sunset* magazine, Menlo Park, California; Richard Brown, Barnet, Vermont; Flora Ann Bynum, Southern Garden History Society, Winston-Salem, North Carolina; Jean Byrne, Pennsylvania Horticultural Society, Philadelphia; Frank Cabot, Cold Spring, New York; Henry Cathey, U.S. National Arboretum, Washington, D.C.; Leslie Close, Wave Hill, New York City; Mary Palmer Dargan, Columbia, South Carolina; Neil Diboll, Prairie Nursery, Westfield, Wisconsin; Charlene Draheim and Christopher Grover, California Redwood Association, Novato, California; Rudy Favretti, Storrs, Connecticut; Viki Ferreniea, Wayside Gardens, Hodges, South Carolina; Nancy Flinn, National Gardening Association, Burlington, Vermont; Lincoln Foster, Falls Village, Connecticut; Carol Greentree, San Diego; Robert E. Grese, University of Michigan; Betsy Gullin, Pennsylvania Horticultural Society, Philadelphia; Lawrence Halprin and Valeri Clarke, San Francisco; J. Drayton Hastie, Magnolia Plantation and Gardens, Charleston, South Carolina; Peter Hatch and John Fitzpatrick, Monticello, Charlottesville, Virginia; Happy Hieronimus, Portland, Oregon; Carol Hollyday, New Canaan, Connecticut; Saxon Holt, San Francisco; Agatha Hughes, Morris Arboretum, Philadelphia; Balthazar and Monica Korab, Troy, Michigan; Michael Laurie, University of California, Berkeley; Carlton Lees, Pittsboro, North Carolina; Sandra Mackenzie Lloyd, Philadelphia; Lee Lockwood, West Newton, Massachusetts; Lothian Lynas, New York Botanical Garden Library; Charles Mann, Plants of the Southwest, Santa Fe, New Mexico; Anne Masury, Strawbery Banke, Portsmouth, New Hampshire; Jim Matheis, Lincoln Memorial Garden, Springfield, Illinois; Bill McDorman and Barbie Reed, High Altitude Gardens, Ketchum, Idaho; Fred and Mary Ann McGourty, Norfolk, Connecticut; Elizabeth McLean, Wynnewood, Pennsylvania; Judy Mielke, Desert Botanical Garden, Phoenix, Arizona; Vicki Moeser, Librarian, Horticultural Society of New York, Carol Ohme, Wenatchee, Washington; Ted Osmundson, San Francisco; Carole Ottesen, Potomac, Maryland; Lorrie Otto, Milwaukee, Wisconsin; Rondal Partridge, San Francisco; Joanne and Jerry Pavia, Portland, Oregon; Bob Perron, Branford, Connecticut; Jane and John Platt, Portland, Oregon; Colvin Randall, Longwood Gardens, Kennett Square, Pennsylvania; Tom Rawls, *Harrowsmith* magazine, Charlotte, Vermont; Pamela Seager, Rancho Los Alamitos Foundation, Long Beach, California; Jack Siebenthaler, Clearwater, Florida; William Tishler, University of Wisconsin; Charles B. Thomas, Lilypons, Maryland; James van Sweden, Washington, D.C.; Michael Van Yahres, Charlottesville, Virginia; Cathy Walker, Chicago; George Waters, Editor, *Pacific Horticulture,* San Francisco; Gail Weesner and Barbara Moore, Beacon Hill Garden Club, Boston; Carol Wishcamper, Freeport, Maine; Leonard Wolfe, Westport, Connecticut; Louisa Wood, Savannah, Georgia; Connie Wyrick, Historic Charleston Foundation, Charleston, South Carolina; and other fellow members of the Garden Writers Association of America, including its executive director, Wil Jung.

Photo Credits

Atlanta Historical Society, 110
Liz Ball, 67 (left); Beacon Hill Garden Club, photo by Southie Burgin, 48 (2), 49, 50 (2), 51; Kurt Bluemel, 89, 92–93, 97 (2), 98, 99 (2); Margaret P. Bowditch, 6 (center), 43 (top), 44 (right), 64–65, 66, 75 (2), 84–85, 87 (top), 92; Brandywine Conservancy/Brandywine River Museum, photo by F. M. Mooberry, 68 (2), 80, 81, 82 (2), 83, 231; © Bob Braun, 128 (left); Judith Bromley, 141 (2), 143 (3); Richard W. Brown, 10 (left), 104 (right), 109, 121, 122 (3), 123, 124, 125 (right); Valerie Brown, 96
California Redwood Association, photo by Ernest Braun, 200, 202; photo by Elyse Lewin, 201; photo by George Lyons, 203; Chicago Botanic Garden, photo by Becky Severson, 29; © Willard Clay, 69, 132–133, 137, 144–45, 235
Michael H. Dodge, 19 (bottom right), 23 (bottom right), 33, 45, 59, 61, 78, 79
© Enrico Ferorelli/DOT, 37 (top left), 38, 176; Richard Fish, 212, 213 (top)
Lawrence Halprin, 192; Richard Hatch, 72, 73; Carrie Hazlegrove, 39, 53; Historic Annapolis William Paca Garden, 77 (top left); © Saxon Holt, 25, 188–189, 194, 195
Bill Irwin & Mal Bernstein, 170
Balthazar Korab, 5, 7 (left), 10 (right), 11 (left), 19 (left), 27, 28 (right), 100–101, 103, 135 (right and bottom), 136, 140, 142, 150

(2), 151, 152, 153, 154, 155, 162 (2), 163 (2); Robert Kourik, 11 (right), 157, 190, 197, 198 (2), 207, 208 (bottom); Carl Kurtz, 102 (top), 108 (left), 134, 164–165, 168–169
Bill Lesche, 186, 187; © Lilypons Water Gardens, 88; Lincoln Memorial Garden and Nature Center, 138, 139; Sandra Mackenzie Lloyd, 86 (2), 87 (bottom left); Ron Lutsko, 208 (top right); © Fred Lyon, 196 (left and top right)
Magnolia Plantation and Gardens, 106–107, 116, 117, 118, 119 (2), 233; Charles Mann, 7 (center), 175 (top right); Steve Martino & Associates Landscape Architects & Planners, 174, 175 (bottom), 182–183, 183; photo by Richard Maack, 181 (bottom), 238; Sylvia Martin, 129 (bottom); Michael McKinley, 147 (bottom left); Elizabeth P. McLean, 12–13, 23 (left and top right), 70–71, 76, 77 (bottom); Margarette Mead, 17 (2); Middleton Place, photo by Terry Richardson, 115; Judy L. Mielke, 166, 167 (bottom left, right), 171, 175 (top left), 181 (top); W. Scott Mitchell, 172, 184, 185 (2)
Nature Conservancy, photo by Susan Bournique, 135 (top left); Richard Nichol, 2–3, 222 (2), 223, 224–225; North Carolina Botanical Garden, photo by Rob Gardner, 111
Brenda Olcott-Reid, 156; Old Salem Village, 15 (left); Carole Ottesen, 91, 95 (2); Lorrie Otto, 146, 147 (top and bottom right)

Jerry Pavia, 206, 208 (left), 209, 211 (bottom), 213 (bottom), 216, 218–219; Joanne Pavia, 26, 191 (right), 215, 217 (2), 218–219; Robert Perron, 36, 37 (bottom left and right), 54; Steve Priebe, 177 (2); © Lanny Provo, 6 (right), 126, 127, 128 (right), 129 (top)
Anne Reed Gallery, 28 (left), 149, 159 (2), 160, 161; Roscoe Village Foundation, photo by Carolyn Hays, 158
Caroline M. Segui, 94; P. R. Singleton, 180; Don B. Stevenson, 167 (top), 171, 173, 178 (2), 179; Thomas R. Stewart, 54–55; Humphrey Sutton, 58 (right), 60, 62 (2), 62–63
George Taloumis, 14, 40, 41 (2); Ogden Tanner, 6 (left), 7 (right), 8–9, 18, 20, 22 (2), 29 (left), 30–31, 32 (2), 34 (2), 35 (2), 42 (2), 43 (bottom), 44 (left), 46 (3), 47, 52, 56 (2), 57, 58 (left), 102 (bottom), 104 (left), 105 (right), 112 (3), 113, 114, 120, 125 (left, bottom), 191 (left), 204–205, 205, 210, 211 (top), 214, 220, 221 (2), 228, 240; Michael Thompson, 87 (bottom right); Bill Tishler, 15 (right); Connie Toops, 105 (left), 108 (right); Tryon Palace Restoration and Gardens Complex, 16
D. L. Vorpahl, 148
Bob Wands for Selby Gardens, 130, 131 (2); L. Wolfe, 67 (right), 74, 77 (top right), 90
Josephine Zeitlin, 21, 24, 193, 196 (bottom right), 199